MW01034167

Donated by Prison Alliance
Write us a letter & enroll in
our PA Bible Study today!
PO Box 97095 Raleigh NC 27624

Register This New Book

Benefits of Registering*

- ✓ FREE **replacements** of lost or damaged books

- ✓ FREE **audiobook** – *Pilgrim's Progress*, audiobook edition

- ✓ FREE information about new titles and other **freebies**

www.anekopress.com/new-book-registration

*See our website for requirements and limitations.

HOW TO STUDY
THE **BIBLE**

ORIGINAL TITLE:
PLEASURE & PROFIT IN BIBLE STUDY

The precepts of the LORD are right, rejoicing the heart; The commandment of the LORD is pure, enlightening the eyes. They are more desirable than gold, yes, than much fine gold; Sweeter also than honey and the drippings of the honeycomb. (Psalm 19:8, 10)

HOW TO STUDY
THE **BIBLE**

Those who love Your law
have great peace, and nothing causes them to stumble.

– Psalm 119:165

D. L. Moody.

ANEKO
PRESS

We love hearing from our readers. Please contact us at www.anekopress.com/questions-comments with any questions, comments, or suggestions.

How to Study the Bible – Dwight L. Moody

Updated Edition Copyright © 2017

First edition published 1895 by Fleming H. Revell Company, Chicago, New York, & Toronto

All rights reserved. No part of this book may be reproduced, stored in a retrieval system, or transmitted in any form or by any means – electronic, mechanical, photocopying, recording, or otherwise, without written permission from the publisher.

Unless otherwise indicated, scripture quotations are taken from the New American Standard Bible® (NASB), copyright © 1960, 1962, 1963, 1968, 1971, 1972, 1973, 1975, 1977, 1995 by The Lockman Foundation. Used by permission. www.Lockman.org.

Cover Design: Natalia Hawthorne, BookCoverLabs.com

Cover Photography: Christophe Testi/Shutterstock

eBook Icon: Icons Vector/Shutterstock

Editors: Paul Miller and Ruth Zetek

Printed in the United States of America

Aneko Press

www.anekopress.com

Aneko Press, Life Sentence Publishing, and our logos are trademarks of

Life Sentence Publishing, Inc.
203 E. Birch Street
P.O. Box 652
Abbotsford, WI 54405

RELIGION / Christian Life / Spiritual Growth

Paperback ISBN: 978-1-62245-456-3

eBook ISBN: 978-1-62245-457-0

10   9   8   7   6   5

Available where books are sold

Contents

Preface

It is always a pleasure to me to speak about studying God's Word. I think I would rather preach about the Word of God than anything else except the love of God, because I believe it is the best thing in the world.

We cannot overestimate the importance of being thoroughly familiar with the Bible. I try to use every opportunity and every means in my power to urge people to constantly study this wonderful Book. If, through the pages that follow, I can reach others and inspire them to read their Bibles, not randomly but with a plan and a purpose, I will indeed be thankful.

When you walk about, they will guide you;
When you sleep, they will watch over you;
And when you awake, they will talk to you.
(Proverbs 6:22)

Chapter 1

No True Life Without the Bible

Aspiritual revitalization that will last must come through the Word of God. A man stood up in one of our meetings and said he hoped to get enough out of the series of meetings to last him all his life. I told him he might as well try to eat enough breakfast at one time to last him his lifetime. That is a mistake that people are making; they are running to religious meetings and thinking the meetings are going to do the work. But if these don't bring you into closer contact with the Word of God, the whole impression will be gone in three months. The more you love the Scriptures, the stronger your faith will be. There is little backsliding when people love the Scriptures. If you come into closer contact with the Word, you will gain something that will last, because the Word of God is going to endure. In Psalm 119, David prayed nine times that God would quicken or strengthen him according to His Word. For example:

> *Revive me according to Your word.*
> (Psalm 119:25)

> *Strengthen me according to Your word.*
> (Psalm 119:28)

> *Revive me, O LORD, according to Your word.* (Psalm 119:107)

> *Sustain me according to Your word.*
> (Psalm 119:116)

If I could say something that would motivate Christians to have a deeper love for the Word of God, I think I would be doing them the most important service that could be done for them. Do you ask, "How can I fall in love with the Bible?" Well, if you will only stir yourself up to study it and ask for God's assistance, He will definitely help you.

Word and work make healthy Christians. If people are all Word and no work, they will suffer from what I may call religious gout. On the other hand, if they are all work and no Word, it will not be long before they will fall into all kinds of sin and error, so that they will do more harm than good. If we first study the Word and then go to work, we will be healthy, useful Christians. I never saw a fruit-bearing Christian who was not a student of the Bible. If a man neglects his Bible, he may pray and ask God to use him in His work, but God cannot use him, for there is not much for the Holy Spirit to work upon. We must have the Word itself, which is sharper than any two-edged sword.

> *For the word of God is living and active and*
> *sharper than any two-edged sword, and*
> *piercing as far as the division of soul and*
> *spirit, of both joints and marrow, and able*
> *to judge the thoughts and intentions of the*
> *heart.* (Hebrews 4:12)

We can have many prayer meetings, but there is something just as important as prayer, and that is that we read our Bibles, that we have Bible study and Bible lectures and Bible classes, so that we may get hold of the Word of God, and that it may get hold of us. When I pray, I talk to God, but when I read the Bible, God is talking to me; and it is really more important that God should speak to me than that I should speak to Him. I believe we would know how to pray better if we knew our Bibles better. What is an army good for if the soldiers don't know how to use their weapons? What is a young man starting out in Christian work good for if he does not know how to use his Bible? A man isn't worth much in battle if he has any doubt about his weapon, and I have never found a man who has doubts about the Bible who has been successful in Christian work. I have seen work after work wrecked because men and women lost confidence in the spirit of this old Book.

> *You shall therefore impress these words*
> *of mine on your heart and on your soul;*
> *and you shall bind them as a sign on your*

> *hand, and they shall be as frontals on*
> *your forehead. You shall teach them to*
> *your sons, talking of them when you sit in*
> *your house and when you walk along the*
> *road and when you lie down and when*
> *you rise up. You shall write them on the*
> *doorposts of your house and on your gates.*
> (Deuteronomy 11:18-20)

If young converts want to be used by God, they must feed on His Word. Their experience may be very good and illuminating at the outset, and they may help others by telling it; but if they keep on doing nothing else but telling their experience, it will soon become stale and unprofitable, and people will get tired of hearing the same thing over and over again. After they have told how they have been converted, the next thing they need to do is feed on the Word. We are not fountains ourselves, but the Word of God is the true fountain.

> *Like newborn babies, long for the pure milk*
> *of the word, so that by it you may grow in*
> *respect to salvation, if you have tasted the*
> *kindness of the Lord.* (1 Peter 2:2-3)

If we feed on the Word of God, it will be easy to speak to others about the Word of God; and not only that, but we will also be growing in grace the entire time, and others will notice the change in our walk and conversation. So few Christians grow, because so few study. I would advise all young converts to spend as much time as they can in the company of more mature Christians. I like to be with those who know more than I do, and I never lose a chance of learning as much as I can from them. Study the Bible carefully and prayerfully; ask others what this passage means and what that passage means, and when you have become familiar with the great truths that the Bible contains, you will have less to fear from the world, the flesh, and the Devil. You will not be disappointed with your Christian life.

> *Be diligent to present yourself approved to God as a workman who does not need to be ashamed, accurately handling the word of truth.* (2 Timothy 2:15)

People are constantly saying, "We want something new. We want some new doctrine or some new idea." Depend upon it, my friends, that if you get tired of the Word of God and it becomes boring to you, you are out of communion with Him.

> *O how I love Your law! it is my meditation all the day.* (Psalm 119:97)

The last time I was in Baltimore, I could see an Episcopal church when I looked out my window. The stained-glass windows were dull and uninviting by day, but when the lights shone through at night, they were beautiful! When the Holy Spirit touches the eyes of your understanding and you see Christ shining through the pages of the Bible, it becomes a new book to you.

> *The precepts of the LORD are right, rejoicing the heart; The commandment of the LORD is pure, enlightening the eyes.* (Psalm 19:8)

A young lady once took up a novel to read, but found it dull and uninteresting. A few months later, she was introduced to the author, and in time became his wife. She then found that there was something exciting and worthwhile in the book, and her opinion of it changed. The change was not in the book, but in herself. She had come to know and love the author.

I will never forget Your precepts, for by
them You have revived me. (Psalm 119:93)

Some Christians read the Bible as a duty, if they read it at all; but as soon as a man or woman sees Christ as the greatest among ten thousand, the Bible becomes the revelation of the Father's love and becomes a never-ending fascination.

A gentleman once asked another man, "Do you often read the Bible?"

"No," was the answer. "I honestly admit I do not love God."

"Neither did I at first," the man replied, "but God loved me."

A great many people seem to think that the Bible is out of date, that it is an old book, and they think it is of no use today. They say it was very good for the Dark Ages and that there is some very good history in it, but it was not intended for the present time; we are living in a very enlightened age and men can get on very well without the old Book; we have outgrown it, they say. Now you might just as well say that the sun, which has shone so long, is now so old that it is out of date, and that whenever a man builds a house

NO TRUE LIFE WITHOUT THE BIBLE

he doesn't need to put any windows in it, because we have a newer light and a better light; we have electric light. But it's not true – nothing can replace the sun's warm rays of light.

> *The grass withers, the flower fades, but the word of our God stands forever.* (Isaiah 40:8)

Keep in mind there is no situation in life for which you cannot find some word of consolation in Scripture. If you are in affliction, if you are in adversity and trial, there is a promise for you. In joy and sorrow, in health and in sickness, in poverty and in riches, in every condition of life, God has a promise stored up in His Word for you. In one way or another, every case is met, and the truth is commended to every man's conscience. It is said that Richard Baxter, author of *The Saints' Everlasting Rest*, was amazed in his youth by the miracles in the Bible; as he grew older, he was more impressed by fulfilled prophecy; and toward the end of his life, he felt the deepest satisfaction in his own sweet experience of the power of the gospel.

- If you are impatient, sit down quietly and commune with Job.

- If you are strong-headed, read about Moses and Peter.

- If you lack courage, look at Elijah.

- If there is no song in your heart, listen to David.

- If you are a politician, read Daniel.

- If you are morally corrupt, read Isaiah.

- If your heart is cold, read of the beloved disciple, John.

- If your faith is low, read Paul.

- If you are getting lazy, learn from James.

- If you are losing sight of the future, read in Revelation of the Promised Land.

In Psalm 119:165, we find these words: *Those who love Your law have great peace, and nothing causes them to stumble.* The study of God's Word will secure peace. Take those Christians who are rooted and grounded in the Word of God, and you will find they have great peace. But those who don't study and who don't know their Bibles are easily offended or discouraged when some little trouble or some little persecution comes, and their peace is all disturbed; just a little breath of opposition, and their peace is all gone.

Sometimes I am amazed to see how little it takes to drive all peace and comfort from some people. A little gossip or slander quickly bothers them; but if we have the peace of God, the world cannot take that peace from us. It cannot give it; it cannot destroy it. We must get it from above the world. It is the peace which only Christ gives. *Those who love Your law have great peace, and nothing causes them to stumble.* Christ says, *And blessed is he who does not take offense at Me* (Matthew 11:6). Wherever there is a Bible-taught Christian, one who has his Bible well marked and who daily feeds upon the Word with prayerful meditation, he will not be easily offended. Those are the people who are growing in Christ and working for Him all the time.

It is the people who never open their Bibles and never study the Scriptures who become offended and discouraged and wonder why they are having such a hard time. They are the people who tell you that Christianity is not what they thought it would be, that it is not as great as we claim it is. The real trouble is that they have not done as the Lord has told them to do. They have neglected the Word of God.

Seek from the book of the LORD, and read.
(Isaiah 34:16)

If they had been studying the Word of God, they would not be in that condition; they would not have wandered away from God all these years, living on the husks of the world. They have neglected to care for the new life. They haven't fed it, and the poor soul, being starved, sinks into weakness and decay, and easily stumbles or is offended. If a man is born of God, he cannot thrive without God.

I met a man who confessed that his soul had fed on nothing for forty years. "Well," said I, "that is pretty hard for the soul – giving it nothing to feed on!" That man is like thousands and tens of thousands today; their poor souls are starving. We take good care of this earthly body that we only have for a short time. We feed it three times a day, and we clothe it, and we dress it, and soon it is going into the grave to rot; but the inner man that is to live on and on forever is weak and starved.

*Man shall not live on bread alone, but on
every word that proceeds out of the mouth
of God.* (Matthew 4:4)

If a man is traveling and does not know where he is
going or how he is going to get there, you know he
is going to have much unnecessary difficulty on his
journey. It is not safe or wise traveling without a plan
and a map. The Bible is a guidebook in the journey of
life, and the only one that points the way to heaven.
Let us take heed then, not to refuse the light and the
help it gives.

*Your word is a lamp to my feet and a light
to my path.* (Psalm 119:105)

Chapter 2

The Word of God Is True

We do not expect men and women to believe in the Bible without looking into it or examining it. It is not natural for us to accept the things of God without question. If you are to *always be ready to make a defense to everyone who asks you to give an account for the hope that is in you* (1 Peter 3:15), you must first ask about it yourself. However, do not be a dishonest doubter, having your heart and mind set against the evidence before you even see it. Do not be a doubter because you think it is intellectual to doubt. Do not cling to your doubts without thinking them through. The German writer Johann Wolfgang von Goethe reportedly said, "Give me the benefit of your convictions, if you have any; but keep your doubts to yourself, for I have enough of my own." Be like Thomas who did not accept Jesus' offer to feel the nail prints in His hands and side; he saw the truth, and his heart was open to change.

> *Then He said to Thomas, Reach here with*
> *your finger, and see My hands; and reach*
> *here your hand and put it into My side;*
> *and do not be unbelieving, but believing.*
> *Thomas answered and said to Him, My*
> *Lord and my God.* (John 20:27-28)

If you are filled with the Word of God, you will not have any doubts about the Word of God. A lady said to me once, "Don't you have any doubts?" No, I don't have time for doubts; there is too much work to be done. Some people live on doubt. It is one of their main characteristics. I believe the reason there are so many Christians who do not show much evidence of walking with God, with whom you only see the Christian graces coming out every now and then, is that they do not take the Bible for doctrine, reproof, and instruction.

> *All Scripture is inspired by God and profitable*
> *for teaching, for reproof, for correction, for*
> *training in righteousness.* (2 Timothy 3:16)

Someone might say to you, "I wish you would prove to me that the Bible is true." The Book will prove itself if you will let it; there is living power in it.

> *For this reason we also constantly thank*
> *God that when you received the word*
> *of God which you heard from us, you*
> *accepted it not as the word of men, but for*
> *what it really is, the word of God, which*
> *also performs its work in you who believe.*
> (1 Thessalonians 2:13)

It does not need defending so much as it needs studying.

It can defend itself. It is not a sick child who needs special care. A Christian man was once talking to a skeptic who said he did not believe the Bible. The man read certain passages to him, but the skeptic said again, "I don't believe a word of it." The man kept on reading, until finally the skeptic was convicted of his sin and of his need for Jesus.

The other man added, "When I have proved a good sword, I keep using it." That is what we need today. It is not our work to make men believe; that is the work of the Holy Spirit.

> *He saved us, not on the basis of deeds which we have done in righteousness, but according to His mercy, by the washing of regeneration and renewing by the Holy Spirit.*
> (Titus 3:5)

A man once sat down to read the Bible for an hour each evening with his wife. After a few evenings, he stopped in the middle of his reading and said, "Wife, if this Book is true, we are wrong." He read on, and before long stopped again and said, "Wife, if this Book is true, we are lost." Riveted to the Book and deeply concerned, he continued to read and soon exclaimed, "Wife, if this Book is true, we may be saved." It was not many days after this that they were both converted. This is the one great end of the Book – to tell us of God's great salvation. Think of it: a book that can lift our troubled spirits and recreate us in God's image!

The law of the LORD is perfect, restoring

*the soul; The testimony of the LORD is sure,
making wise the simple.* (Psalm 19:7)

It is a serious responsibility to have God's Word and yet
neglect its warnings and reject its teachings. Following
the Word of God results in life, but rejecting it results
in death. What if God should take His Word away and
say, "I will not trouble you with it anymore"?

*How will we escape if we neglect so great
a salvation? After it was at the first spoken
through the Lord, it was confirmed to us by
those who heard.* (Hebrews 2:3)

You might wonder what you should do when you come
to a part of the Bible that you cannot understand. I
thank God there is a height in that Book I do not know
anything about, and a depth I have never been able to
fathom, and it makes the Book all the more fascinating. If I could take that Book and read it as I can any
other book and understand it in one reading, I would
have lost faith in it years ago. It is one of the strongest
proofs that the Book must have come from God, that
the wisest men who have studied the Bible for fifty
years have laid down their pens and said, "There is
much more yet to learn from that Book."

"No Scripture," said Spurgeon, "is exhausted by a
single explanation. The flowers of God's garden bloom,
not only double, but sevenfold; they are continually
pouring forth fresh fragrance."

A man came to me with a difficult passage some
time ago and said, "Moody, what do you do with that?"

"I do not do anything with it."

"How do you understand it?"

"I don't understand it."

"How do you explain it?"

"I do not explain it."

"What do you do with it?"

"I do not do anything."

"You do not believe it, do you?"

"Oh yes, I believe it."

There are lots of things I do not understand, but I believe them. I do not know anything about higher mathematics, but I believe in them. I do not understand astronomy, but I believe in astronomy. Can you tell me why the same kind of food turns into flesh, fish, hair, feathers, hooves, or fingernails – depending upon which animal eats that food? A man told me a while ago he could not believe a thing he had never seen. I said, "Man, did you ever see your brain?"

Dr. Thomas Talmage tells the story that one day while he was bothering his theological professor with questions about the mysteries of the Bible, the latter turned on him and said, "Mr. Talmage, you will have to let God know some things you don't."

A man once said to an infidel, "The mysteries of the Bible don't bother me. I read the Bible as I eat fish. When I am eating fish and come across a bone, I don't try to swallow it; I lay it aside. And when I am reading the Bible and come across something I can't understand, I say, 'There is a bone,' and I pass it by. But I don't throw the fish away because of the bones in it; and I don't throw my Bible away because of a few passages I can't explain."

Pascal said, "Human knowledge must be understood in order to be loved, but divine knowledge must be loved to be understood." That marks the point of failure of most critics of the Bible. They do not make their brain the servant of their heart.

Did you ever notice that the things in the Bible that people object to the most are the very things to which Christ has set His seal? They say, "You don't believe in the story of Noah and the flood, do you?" Well, if I give up that story, then I must give up the gospel; I must give up the teachings of Jesus Christ. Christ believed in the story of Noah, and connected that with His return to earth. *And just as it happened in the days of Noah, so it will be also in the days of the Son of Man* (Luke 17:26).

People say, "You don't believe in the story of Lot and Sodom, do you?" Yes, I do, just as much as I believe the teachings of Jesus Christ. *Likewise also as it was the same as happened in the days of Lot; It will be just the same on the day that the Son of Man is revealed* (Luke 17:28a, 30).

Scoffers say, "You don't believe in the story of Lot's wife, do you?" Christ believed it. *Remember Lot's wife* (Luke 17:32).

"You don't believe the story of Israel looking to a brass serpent for deliverance, do you?" Christ believed it and connected it with His own cross. *As Moses lifted up the serpent in the wilderness, even so must the Son of Man be lifted up; so that whoever believes will in Him have eternal life* (John 3:14-15).

They say, "You don't believe the children of Israel were fed with manna in the desert, do you?" *Our fathers ate the manna in the wilderness; as it is written, He gave them bread out of heaven to eat. Jesus then said to them, Truly, truly, I say to you, it is not Moses who has given you the bread out of heaven, but it is My Father who gives you the true bread out of heaven* (John 6:31-32).

People say, "Do you believe they drank water that came out of a rock?" Christ believed it. *Then Moses lifted up his hand and struck the rock twice with his rod; and water came forth abundantly, and the congregation and their beasts drank* (Numbers 20:11).

Scorners say, "You don't believe in the story of Elijah being fed by the widow, do you?" Certainly. Christ said that many widows were in Israel in the days of Elijah, but Elijah was fed by only one widow (Luke 4:25-26). Christ referred to it Himself. He set His seal to it. The Son of God believed it, and will the disciple be above his master (Luke 6:40)?

They say, "Well, you don't believe in the story of Jonah and the whale, do you?" I want to tell you I *do* believe it. A few years ago, there was a man who someone thought was a little unsound, and they didn't want him to preach at our Northfield church. I said, "I will soon find out whether or not he is sound."

I asked him, "Do you believe that the fish swallowed Jonah?"

"Yes," he said, "I do."

I said, "All right then. I want you to come and speak." He came and gave a lecture on Jonah. In Matthew, Jesus was asked twice for a sign, and He said the only sign this generation would have would be the sign of Jonah in the fish's belly (Matthew 12:39-40; 16:4).

For just as Jonah was three days and three nights in the belly of the sea monster, so will the Son of Man be three days and three nights in the heart of the earth.
(Matthew 12:40)

Jesus connected that with His resurrection, and I honestly believe that if we overthrow the one, we must overthrow the other. As you get along in life and have perhaps as many friends on the other side of the river as you have on this side, you will get about as much comfort out of the story of the resurrection as any other story in the Bible. Christ had no doubt about the story. He said His resurrection would be a sign like that given unto the Ninevites. It was the resurrected man, Jonah, who walked through the streets of Nineveh. The men of Nineveh had probably heard about Jonah being thrown overboard and swallowed by a great fish.

I think it is a masterstroke of Satan to make us doubt the resurrection, but these modern philosophers have made a discovery. They say a whale's throat is no larger than a man's fist, and that it is a physical impossibility for a whale to swallow a man. The book of Jonah says that *the LORD appointed a great fish to swallow Jonah* (Jonah 1:17). Couldn't God make a fish large enough to swallow Jonah? If God could create a world, and all the animals on it, I think He could create a fish large enough to swallow a million men. As one woman said, "Could He not, if He chose, prepare a man that could swallow a whale?"

> *But Jesus answered and said to them,*
> *You are mistaken, not understand-*
> *ing the Scriptures nor the power of God.*
> (Matthew 22:29)

A couple of these modern philosophers were sailing to Europe some time ago, and a Scotch friend of mine was on board who knew his Bible pretty well. They began talking about the Bible, and one of them said, "I am a scientific man, and I have made some investigation of that Book, and I have looked at some of the statements in it, examined them, and I declare them to be false. There is a statement in the Bible that Balaam's donkey spoke. I have taken pains to examine the mouth of a donkey, and it is so formed that it could not speak."

My friend stood it as long as he could and then said, "Well, sir, you make the donkey, and I will make him speak." The idea that God could not speak through the mouth of a donkey!

> *And the LORD opened the mouth of the*
> *donkey, and she said to Balaam, What have*
> *I done to you, that you have struck me these*
> *three times? Then the LORD opened the*
> *eyes of Balaam, and he saw the angel of the*
> *LORD standing in the way with his drawn*
> *sword in his hand; and he bowed all the*
> *way to the ground.* (Numbers 22:28, 31)

Chapter 3

All of God's Word Is True

There is another class of people that only wants to believe part of the Bible. It is quite popular for people to say, "Yes, I believe the Bible, but not the supernatural parts. I believe everything based upon reason." They go on reading the Bible with a pocket-knife, cutting out this and that. Now, if I have a right to cut out a certain portion of the Bible, I don't know why one of my friends has not a right to cut out another, and another friend to cut out another part, and so on. You would have a strange kind of Bible if everybody cut out what he wanted to. Every adulterer would cut out everything about adultery; every liar would cut out everything about lying; every drunkard would be cutting out what he didn't like.

You invalidated the word of God for the sake of your tradition. You hypocrites, rightly did Isaiah prophesy of you: This

*people honors me with their lips, but their
heart is far away from me. But in vain do
they worship me, teaching as doctrines the
precepts of men.* (Matthew 15:6-9)

A gentleman once took his Bible to his minister and said, "This is your Bible."

"Why do you call it *my* Bible?" asked the minister.

"Well," replied the gentleman, "I have been sitting under your preaching for five years, and whenever you said that something in the Bible was not true, I cut it out." He had about a third of the Bible cut out: all of Job, all of Ecclesiastes and Revelation, and a good deal more. The minister wanted him to leave the Bible with him; he didn't want the rest of his congregation to see it. But the man said, "Oh no! I still have the covers left, and I will hold on to them." And off he went, holding on to the covers.

If you believed what some men preach, you would have nothing but the covers left in a few months. I have often said that if I am going to throw away the Bible, I will throw it all into the fire at once. There is no need of waiting five years to do what you can do just as well at once. I have yet to find a man who begins to pick at the Bible who does not pick it all to pieces in a little while.

I met a minister a while ago who said to me, "Moody, I have given up preaching except out of the four Gospels. I no longer preach from the New Testament Epistles or any of the Old Testament; I don't know why I cannot just go to the source and preach as Paul did. I believe the Gospels are all there is that is authentic." It was not long before he gave up the four Gospels too, and finally gave up the ministry. He gave up the Bible, and God gave him up.

Every word of God is tested. (Proverbs 30:5)

A prophet who had been sent to a city to warn the wicked was commanded not to eat meat within the city's walls. He was afterwards deceived into doing so by an old prophet, who told him that an angel had come to him and told him that he could return and eat with him. That prophet was destroyed by a lion for his disobedience (1 Kings 13). If an angel should come and tell a different story from that in the Book, don't believe it. I am sick and tired of people following men. It is written: *But even if we, or an angel from heaven, should preach to you a gospel contrary to what we have preached to you, he is to be accursed* (Galatians 1:8). Do you think that we can disobey God's Word with impunity when we have more light before us than that prophet had?

> *But the word is very near you, in your mouth and in your heart, that you may observe it. See, I have set before you today life and prosperity, and death and adversity; in that I command you today to love the LORD your God, to walk in His ways and to keep His commandments and His statutes and His judgments, that you may live and multiply, and that the LORD your God may bless you in the land where you are entering to possess it. But if your heart*

*turns away and you will not obey, but are
drawn away and worship other gods and
serve them, I declare to you today that
you shall surely perish. You will not pro-
long your days in the land where you are
crossing the Jordan to enter and possess it.*
(Deuteronomy 30:14-18)

It is a most absurd statement for someone to say he
will have nothing to do with the miracles and will
not believe the supernatural. If you are going to reject
the supernatural, you might as well burn your Bibles
at once. If you take the supernatural out of that Book,
you have taken Jesus Christ out of it; you have taken out
the best part of the Book. There is no part of the Bible
that does not teach supernatural things. In Genesis
it says that Abraham fell on his face and God talked
with him. That is supernatural. If that did not take
place, then the man who wrote Genesis wrote a lie, and
out goes Genesis. In Exodus you find the ten plagues
which came upon Egypt. If that is not true, then the
writer of Exodus was a liar. Then in Leviticus it is said
that fire consumed the two sons of Aaron. That was a
supernatural event, and if that was not true, then we
must throw out the whole Book.

*Then the LORD said to Moses, Say to
Aaron, Stretch out your staff and strike the
dust of the earth, that it may become gnats
through all the land of Egypt. They did so;
and Aaron stretched out his hand with his
staff, and struck the dust of the earth, and*

*there were gnats on man and beast. All
the dust of the earth became gnats through
all the land of Egypt. The magicians tried
with their secret arts to bring forth gnats,
but they could not; so there were gnats
on man and beast. Then the magicians
said to Pharaoh, This is the finger of God.*
(Exodus 8:16-19a)

In Numbers is the story of the bronze serpent. And so with every book in the Old Testament; there is not one in which you do not find something supernatural. The Gospels contain more supernatural things than any other portion of the Bible, and the last thing a man is willing to give up is the four Gospels, about Jesus Christ. Five hundred years before His birth, the angel Gabriel came down and told Daniel that He would be born: *While I was still speaking in prayer, then the man Gabriel, whom I had seen in the vision previously, came to me in my extreme weariness about the time of the evening offering* (Daniel 9:21). Again, Gabriel came down to Nazareth and told the virgin Mary that she would be the mother of the Savior. *The angel said to her, Do not be afraid, Mary; for you have found favor with God. And behold, you will conceive in your womb and bear a son, and you shall name Him Jesus* (Luke 1:30-31).

We find too that the angel went into the temple and told Zacharias that he was to be the father of John the Baptist, the forerunner of the Messiah; Zacharias was struck mute for nine months because of his unbelief (Luke 1:5-25). Then when Christ was born, we find angels appearing to the shepherds at Bethlehem, telling them of the birth of the Savior: *But the angel said to them, Do not be afraid; for behold, I bring you good news of great joy which will be for all the people; for today in the city of David there has been born for you a Savior, who is Christ the Lord* (Luke 2:10-11).

The wise men seeing the star in the east and following it was surely supernatural (Matthew 2:1-12). So was the warning that God sent to Joseph in a dream, telling him to flee to Egypt (Matthew 2:13). So was the fact of our Lord going into the temple at the age of twelve, discussing with the scholars, and being a match for them all (Luke 2:46-49). So were the circumstances regarding His baptism, when God spoke from heaven.

> *After being baptized, Jesus came up immediately from the water; and behold, the heavens were opened, and he saw the Spirit of God descending as a dove and lighting on Him, and behold, a voice out of the heavens said, This is My beloved Son, in whom I am well-pleased.* (Matthew 3:16-17)

For three and a half years, Jesus trod the streets and highways of Israel. Think of the many wonderful miracles that He performed during those years. One day He spoke to the leper, and the leper was made whole. Another day He spoke to the sea, and it obeyed Him. When He died, the sun refused to look upon the scene; this old world recognized Him and reeled and rocked like a drunken man. When He broke open the bands of death and came out of Joseph's sepulchre, that was supernatural.

In his sermon "The Time of Reformation," Christmas Evans, the great Welsh preacher, said, "Many reformations have expired with the reformers. But our Great Reformer 'ever liveth' to carry on His reformation, till His enemies become His footstool, and death and hell are cast into the lake of fire." Thank God we do not worship a dead Jew. If we worshipped a dead Jew, we would not have been made alive and received life in our souls. I thank God that our Christ is a supernatural Christ and that this Book is a supernatural Book; and I thank God that I live in a country where it is so free that all people can read it.

Some people think we are deluded, that this is imagination. Well, it is a glorious imagination, is it not? It has lasted between thirty and forty years with me, and I think it is going to last while I am still living and continue on when I go into another world.

When Paul wrote to Timothy that *all* Scripture was given by inspiration of God and was profitable (2 Timothy 3:16), he meant what he said. "Well," some say, "do you believe all Scripture is given by inspiration?" Yes, every word of it; but I don't believe all the actions and incidents it tells of were inspired. For instance, when the Devil told a lie, he was not inspired to tell a lie, and when a wicked man like Ahab said anything, he was not inspired; but someone was inspired to write it, and so all was given by inspiration and is profitable.

Inspiration must have been verbal in many, if not in

all, cases. Regarding salvation through the sufferings of Christ, Peter tells us:

> *As to this salvation, the prophets who prophesied of the grace that would come to you made careful searches and inquiries, seeking to know what person or time the Spirit of Christ within them was indicating as He predicted the sufferings of Christ and the glories to follow. It was revealed to them that they were not serving themselves, but you, in these things which now have been announced to you through those who preached the gospel to you by the Holy Spirit sent from heaven -things into which angels long to look.* (1 Peter 1:10-12)

The prophets themselves had to inquire and search diligently regarding the words they uttered under the inspiration of the Spirit.

A man said to a young convert, "How can you prove that the Bible is inspired?"

He replied, "Because it inspires me."

I think that is pretty good proof. Let the Word of God into your soul, and it will inspire you; it cannot help it.

> *Is not My word like fire? declares the LORD, and like a hammer which shatters a rock?* (Jeremiah 23:29)

Chapter 4

Don't Neglect the Old Testament

I want to show how absurd it is for people to say they believe the New Testament but not the Old Testament. It is a very interesting fact that of the thirty-nine books in the Old Testament, our Lord quoted from no less than twenty-two of them. He may very well have quoted from all of them, for the Gospels only contain a small part of what He said and did. The apostle John tells us that the world could scarcely contain the books that could be written if all the sayings and actions of our Lord were recorded. About 850 passages in the Old Testament are quoted or alluded to in the New, with only a few occurring more than once.

> *And there are also many other things which*
> *Jesus did, which if they were written in*
> *detail, I suppose that even the world itself*

would not contain the books that would be written. (John 21:25)

In the gospel of Matthew, there are over 100 quotations from twenty Old Testament books. In the gospel of Mark, there are fifteen quotations taken from thirteen of the Old Testament books. In the gospel of Luke, there are thirty-four quotations from thirteen books. In the gospel of John, there are eleven quotations from six books. In the four Gospels alone, there are more than 160 quotations from the Old Testament. You sometimes hear men saying they do not believe all the Bible, but they believe the teachings of Jesus Christ in the four Gospels. Well, if I believe that, I have to accept these 160 quotations from the Old Testament. In Paul's letter to the Corinthians, there are fifty-three quotations from the Old Testament; sometimes he takes whole paragraphs from it. In the thirteen chapters of the book of Hebrews, there are eighty-five quotations from the Old Testament. In Galatians, there are sixteen quotations. In the book of Revelation alone, there are 245 quotations and allusions.

A great many people want to throw out the Old Testament. It is good historic reading, they say, but they do not believe it is a part of the Word of God, and they don't regard it as essential in the scheme of salvation. The last letter Paul wrote contained the following words: *and that from childhood you have known the sacred writings which are able to give you the wisdom that leads to salvation through faith which is in Christ Jesus* (2 Timothy 3:15). The Scriptures which the apostles possessed were the Old Testament.

When skeptics attack the truths of the Old Testament, some Christians find it convenient to say, "Well, we don't endorse all that is in the Old Testament," and thus they avoid an argument in defense of the Scriptures. It is very important that every Christian should know and accept what the Old Testament teaches, because it is upon this that truth is based. Peter said the Scriptures were not given by any private interpretation, and when he wrote of the Scriptures, he was referring to the Old Testament.

> So we have the prophetic word made more sure, to which you do well to pay attention as to a lamp shining in a dark place, until the day dawns and the morning star arises in your hearts. But know this first of all, that no prophecy of Scripture is a matter of one's own interpretation, for no prophecy was ever made by an act of human will, but men moved by the Holy Spirit spoke from God. (2 Peter 1:19-21)

If the Old Testament Scriptures are not true, do you think Christ would have so often referred to them and said that the Scriptures must be fulfilled?

> Now He said to them, These are My words which I spoke to you while I was still with you, that all things which are written about Me in the Law of Moses and the Prophets and the Psalms must be fulfilled. (Luke 24:44)

When told by the tempter that He could call down the angels from heaven to intercede on His behalf, Jesus said, "But how then shall the scriptures be fulfilled that thus it must be? (Matthew 26:54). Christ gave Himself up as a sacrifice so that the Scriptures would be fulfilled. He was numbered with the transgressors (Mark 15:28; Luke 22:37). When He talked with two of His disciples on the way to Emmaus after His resurrection, He asked them, *was it not necessary for the Christ to suffer these things and to enter into His glory?* (Luke 24:26). Luke adds: *Then beginning with Moses and with all the prophets, He explained to them the things concerning Himself in all the Scriptures* (Luke 24:27), for the one theme of the Old Testament is the Messiah.

Psalm 40:7 says, *In the scroll of the book it is written of me.* "What Book?" asks Martin Luther, "and what Person? There is only one book – the Bible; and only one person – Jesus Christ." Christ referred to the Scriptures and their fulfillment in Him, not only after He arose from the dead, but in heaven too, according to the book of Revelation. He spoke of them to John on the Isle of Patmos, and used the very things in the Scriptures that men are now trying to reject. Jesus never found fault with or rejected the Old Testament.

If Jesus Christ could use the Old Testament, let us use it. May God deliver us from the one-sided Christian who reads only the New Testament and talks against the Old!

Chapter 5

God's Word Endures Forever

Christ, speaking of the law, said, *not the smallest letter or stroke shall pass from the Law until all is accomplished* (Matthew 5:18). In another place He said, *Heaven and earth will pass away, but My words will not pass away* (Matthew 24:35). Now, let us keep in mind that the only Scripture the apostles and Christ had was the Old Testament. The New Testament was not yet written. We can also call them the old and new covenants. *Not the smallest letter or stroke shall pass from the Law until all is accomplished* – the old covenant; and then Christ comes and adds these words: *Heaven and earth will pass away, but My words will not pass away* – the new covenant.

Notice how that has been fulfilled. There was no reporter following Him around writing down His words. There were no papers to print the sermons, and they wouldn't have printed His sermons if there had been any daily papers; the whole church and all the religious world were against Him. I can imagine one of your modern freethinkers standing near Him, and he hears Christ say, *Heaven and earth will pass away, but My words will not pass away.* I see the scornful look on his face as he says, "Hear that Jewish peasant talk! Did you ever hear such conceit, such insanity? He says heaven and earth will pass away, but His words will not pass away."

My friend, I want to ask you this question: have they passed away? There are more Bibles today than ever before in the history of the world. There have been more Bibles printed in the last ten years than in the previous eighteen hundred years. They tried in the Dark Ages to chain the Bible and keep it from the nations, but God has preserved it, and the British and American Bible societies print thousands of Bibles every day. One publishing house in New York sold one hundred thousand Oxford Bibles last year.

Notwithstanding all that skeptics and infidels say against the old Book, it continues to prosper. These objectors remind me of a dog barking at the moon; the moon goes on shining just the same. Atheists keep on writing against the Bible, but they do not make much progress, do they? It is being spread all abroad, silently, and without any blasts of trumpets. The lighthouse does not blow a trumpet; it goes on shining its light all around. So the Bible is lighting up the nations of the earth. It is said that a lecturer on secularism was once asked, "Why can't you let the Bible alone if you don't believe it?" The honest reply was at once made: "Because the Bible won't let me alone."

The Bible was about the first book ever printed, and today, New Testaments are printed in 353 different languages and are going to the very corners of the earth.[1] Wherever the Bible has not been translated, the people have no literature. It will not be long before the words of Jesus Christ will penetrate the darkest parts of the earth and the darkest islands of the sea. When Christ said *the Scripture cannot be broken* (John 10:35), He meant every word He said. The Devil and man and hell have been united for centuries in trying to destroy the Word of God, but they cannot do it. If you can stand on the Word of God, you have good footing for time and eternity. *Heaven and earth will pass away, but My words will not pass away.* My friends, that Word is going to live, and there is no power in hell or on earth that can destroy it.

We need people today who believe in the Bible from the crown of their heads to the soles of their feet. We need people who believe the whole of it – the things they understand, and the things they do not understand. Talk about the things you understand, and accept the things you do not. We need to study the whole Bible. There are a good many Christians who are familiar with one book of the Bible, but do not know the rest of the Bible. When I went to Scotland, I had to be very careful how I quoted the Bible. They seemed to know all of the Bible there, and someone would tell me after the meeting if I quoted a verse wrong.

---

1   According to Wycliffe Bible Translators, as of 2015, more than 1,300 languages have access to the New Testament and some portions of Scripture in their language. More than 550 languages have the complete translated Bible. Up to 180 million people still need Bible translation to begin in their language (*www.wycliffe.org/about/why*).

Chapter 6

Accurate Yesterday, Today, and Tomorrow

I know nothing that will upset an honest skeptic quicker than fulfilled prophecy. There are very few Christians who think of studying this subject. They say that prophecies are mysterious, and it is sometimes difficult to be certain that they have been fulfilled. The Bible does not say that prophecy is a difficult subject to be avoided, but rather that *We have the prophetic word made more sure, to which you do well to pay attention as to a lamp shining in a dark place, until the day dawns and the morning star arises in your hearts* (2 Peter 1:19). Prophecy is history unfulfilled, and history is prophecy fulfilled.

When I was a boy, I was taught that everything beyond the Mississippi River was the great American desert. But when the first pickax struck into the Comstock lode and they took out more than one hundred million dollars' worth of silver, the nation realized that there was no desert; and today that part of the country – Nevada, Colorado, Utah, and other western states – is some of the most valuable we possess. Think of the busy cities and flourishing states that have sprung up among the mountains! So it is with many portions of the Bible, but people never think of reading them. They are living on only a few verses and chapters. The greater part of the Bible was written by prophets, yet you do not often hear a sermon on prophecy.

Between five and six hundred Old Testament prophecies have been remarkably and literally fulfilled, and two hundred in regard to Jesus Christ alone. Not a thing happened to Jesus Christ that was not prophesied from seventeen hundred to four hundred years before He was born.

The prophets also spoke about nations and cities. Take the four great cities that existed in the days when the Old Testament was written, and you will find that prophecies regarding them have been fulfilled to the letter. Let me call your attention to a few passages.

First, regarding Babylon:

And Babylon, the beauty of kingdoms, the glory of the Chaldeans' pride, will be as when God overthrew Sodom and Gomorrah. It will never be inhabited or lived in from generation to generation; Nor will the Arab pitch his tent there, nor will shepherds make their flocks lie down there. But desert creatures will lie down there, and their houses will be full of owls; Ostriches also will live there, and shaggy goats will frolic there. Hyenas will howl in their fortified towers and jackals in their luxurious palaces. Her fateful time also will soon come and her days will not be prolonged. (Isaiah 13:19-22)

And again:

The word which the LORD spoke concerning Babylon, the land of the Chaldeans, through Jeremiah the prophet: Declare and proclaim among the nations. Proclaim it and lift up a standard. Do not conceal it but say, Babylon has been captured, Bel has been put to shame, Marduk has been shattered; Her images have been put to shame, her idols have been shattered. For a nation has come up against her out of the north; it will make her land an object of horror, and there will be no inhabitant in it. Both man and beast have wandered off, they have gone away. Because of the indignation of the LORD she will not be inhabited, but she will be completely desolate; Everyone who passes by Babylon will be horrified and will hiss because of all her wounds. How the hammer of the whole earth has been cut off and broken! How Babylon has become an object of horror among the nations! I set a snare for you and you were also caught, O Babylon, while you yourself were not aware; You have been found and also seized because

you have engaged in conflict with the LORD.
(Jeremiah 50:1-3, 13, 23-24)

A hundred years before Nebuchadnezzar ascended the throne, God's prophets foretold how Babylon would be destroyed, and it came to pass. Scholars tell us that the city stood in the middle of a large and fruitful plain. It was enclosed by a wall sixty miles in circumference. Each side of the square had twenty gates of solid brass, and at every corner was a strong tower, ten feet higher than the wall. The wall was eighty-seven feet broad and three hundred and fifty feet high. These figures give us an idea of the importance of Babylon, yet nothing but ruins now remain to tell of its former grandeur. When Babylon was in its glory and was known as the queen of the earth, prophets predicted that it would be destroyed; how literally it was fulfilled!

A friend going through the valley of the Euphrates tried to get his guide to pitch his tent near the ruins, but the guide would not stay there.

Now take Nineveh:

> *I will throw filth on you and make you vile,*
> *and set you up as a spectacle. And it will*
> *come about that all who see you will shrink*
> *from you and say, Nineveh is devastated!*
> *Who will grieve for her? Where will I seek*
> *comforters for you?* (Nahum 3:6-7)

Now, how are you going to cover up the city? *I will throw filth on you.* How are you going to throw filth upon the city? For twenty-five hundred years, Nineveh was buried and an abominable filth lay upon her, but now they have dug up the ruins and brought them to Paris and London. You can go into the British Museum, and people from all over the world are there looking at the artifacts from the ruins of Nineveh. It is just as the prophets prophesied. For twenty-five hundred years, Nineveh was buried; but it is no longer buried.

Then look at Tyre:

> *Therefore thus says the Lord GOD, Behold, I am against you, O Tyre, and I will bring up many nations against you, as the sea brings up its waves. They will destroy the walls of Tyre and break down her towers; and I will scrape her debris from her and make her a bare rock. She will be a place for the spreading of nets in the midst of the sea, for I have spoken, declares the Lord GOD, and she will become spoil for the nations.* (Ezekiel 26:3-5)

Charles Coffin, who was a correspondent for the *Boston Journal* during the Civil War, travelled around the world in 1868, after the war was over. One night he came to the site of old Tyre, and he said the sun was just going down, and he got his guide to pitch his tent right over by the ruins, where the rocks were scraped bare. Coffin took out his Bible and read where it says, *She will be a place for the spreading of nets.* He said the fishermen were done fishing and were just spreading their nets on the rocks of Tyre, precisely as it was prophesied hundreds and hundreds of years before. Remember, when they prophesied against these great cities, the cities were like London, Paris, and New York in their glory; but their glory has gone.

Now take the prophecy regarding Jerusalem:

> *When He approached Jerusalem, He saw*
> *the city and wept over it, saying, If you had*
> *known in this day, even you, the things*
> *which make for peace! But now they have*
> *been hidden from your eyes. For the days*
> *will come upon you when your enemies will*
> *throw up a barricade against you, and sur-*
> *round you and hem you in on every side.*
> (Luke 19:41-43)

Didn't Titus do that? Didn't the Roman emperor do that very thing? It also happened as Jesus said next: *and they will level you to the ground and your children within you, and they will not leave in you one stone upon another, because you did not recognize the time of your visitation* (Luke 19:44).

I have read of two rabbis who went up to Jerusalem and saw a fox playing upon the wall. One rabbi began to weep when he saw the desolation of Zion. The other rabbi smiled and rebuked him, saying that this was proof that the Word of God was true, and that this was one of the prophecies that would be fulfilled: *Because of Mount Zion which lies desolate, foxes prowl in it* (Lamentations 5:18). It was also said that Jerusalem would be as a plowed field (Micah 3:12). This prophecy has also been fulfilled. The modern city is so restricted that outside of the walls, where part of the old city stood, the plow has been used.

Now take the prophecies regarding Egypt:

> *It will be the lowest of the kingdoms, and*
> *it will never again lift itself up above the*
> *nations. And I will make them so small*
> *that they will not rule over the nations.*
> (Ezekiel 29:15)

Egypt was in its glory when this was prophesied. It was a great and mighty empire, but has since lost its glory.

Now look at prophecies regarding the Jewish people:

The prophecy of Balaam with regard to the Jews has been already greatly fulfilled: *behold, a people who dwells apart, and will not be reckoned among the nations. Who can count the dust of Jacob, or number the fourth part of Israel?* (Numbers 23:9-10).

Many people did not want the Jews to be counted among the nations. There is something in this people's looks and habits, though, that God continues to perpetuate, and they are witnesses in every land of the truth of the Bible.

The Jewish race has remained all these centuries separate and distinct from other nations. In America, there are all kinds of nationalities, but the Jew is as much a Jew as he was when he came over here one hundred years ago. See how the race has been persecuted, yet the Jews cannot be kept down. Egypt, Edom, Assyria, Babylon, Persia, Rome, and all the leading nations of the earth have sought to crush the Jews. Frederick the Great said, "Touch them not, for no one has done so and prospered."

*Now the LORD said to Abram, Go forth
from your country, and from your relatives
and from your father's house, to the land
which I will show you; And I will make you
a great nation, and I will bless you, and
make your name great; And so you shall
be a blessing; And I will bless those who
bless you, and the one who curses you I
will curse. And in you all the families of the
earth will be blessed.* (Genesis 12:1-3)

The people are the same now as they were in the days
of Pharaoh, when he tried to destroy all the male children (Exodus 1:15-22). The prophecy is fulfilled. God
has made the nation numerous and united. The time
is coming when God will reinstate the Jews.[2] *For the
sons of Israel will remain for many days without king
or prince, without sacrifice or sacred pillar and without ephod or household idols* (Hosea 3:4). Are they not
without a king, without a nation, and without a sacrifice? Are they not scattered among the nations of the
earth, a separate and distinct people? And they do not
bow down to idols. They crucified their last King, and
they will never have another until they restore Him.
He was Jesus Christ, as inscribed upon His cross, "The
King of the Jews."

*Pilate also wrote an inscription and put it
on the cross. It was written, JESUS THE
NAZARENE, THE KING OF THE JEWS.*
(John 19:19)

---

2   Moody wrote this, of course, before 1948, when Israel again became
a nation.

There are many other prophecies in the Bible. We see how it was prophesied that Eli was going to suffer (1 Samuel 2:27-36). He was God's own high priest, and the only thing against him was that he did not obey God's word faithfully and diligently. He was like a good many people nowadays. He was one of these good-natured old men who don't want to make people uncomfortable by saying unpleasant things, so he let his two boys go on in sin and did not restrain them. He was just like some ministers. Oh! let every minister tell the truth, even if he should preach himself out of favor with his people. Everything went all right for twenty years, but then came fulfillment of the prophecy. God's ark was taken, and the army of Israel was routed by the Philistines. Hophni and Phinehas, old Eli's two sons, were killed, and when the old man heard of it, he fell back in his chair, broke his neck, and died.

So it was with King Ahab taking the sinful advice of Jezebel. Naboth would not sell him that piece of land, so they got him out of the way. Three years afterwards, the dogs licked Ahab's blood from his chariot in the very spot where Naboth's blood had been murderously shed (1 Kings 21:19; 22:34-38).

Chapter 7

Give Them God's Word

Here is a word of counsel for young men who have their eye on the ministry. If you take my advice, you will not make your sermons from random texts, but will preach straight through a book of the Bible. I believe that what this country needs is the Word of God. There is no book that will draw people in like the Bible. One of the professors at a university in Chicago gave some lectures on the book of Job, and there was no building large enough to hold the people. If the Bible has a chance to speak for itself, it will interest the people. I am sick and tired of moral essays. It would take about a ton of them to convert a child five years old.

A man was talking about a certain church once, and he said he liked it because the preacher never talked about politics and religion, but he just read nice little essays. Give the people the Word of God. Some men only use the Bible as a book of texts. They get a text and away they go. They start out by reading a verse or two from the Bible, and then they start talking about their own topics and never get around to preaching what God's Word says. They talk about astronomy and geology, add some news or entertainment, and next Sunday they go on in the same way, and then they wonder why it is that people do not read their Bibles.

I used to think Charles Spurgeon was about as good a preacher as I ever knew, but I would rather hear him explain the Scriptures than listen to all his sermons. Why is it that Dr. John Hall has had his congregation so long? He opens his Bible and expounds. How was it that Andrew Bonar kept his audience in Glasgow? He had a weak voice and people could hardly hear him, yet thirteen hundred people would file into his church twice every Sabbath. Many of them took notes, and they would go home and send his sermons all over the world. It was Dr. Bonar's custom to lead his congregation through the study of the Bible, book by book. There was not a part of the Bible in which he could not find Christ. I preached five months in Glasgow, and there was not a ward or a district in the city in which I did not find the influence of that man.

I was in London in 1884 and a respected lawyer had come down from Edinburgh. He said he went to Glasgow a few weeks before to spend a Sunday there, and he was fortunate enough to hear Andrew Bonar. He said he happened to be there the Sunday Dr. Bonar got to that part of the epistle of Galatians where it says that Paul went up to Jerusalem to see Peter. *Then three years later I went up to Jerusalem to become acquainted with Cephas, and stayed with him fifteen days* (Galatians 1:18).

Dr. Bonar then let his imagination roam, the lawyer told me. Bonar said that he could imagine that Peter and Paul had been very busy one day and they were tired, and all at once, Peter turned to Paul and said, "Paul, wouldn't you like to take a little walk?" And Paul said he would.

So they went down through the streets of Jerusalem, over the brook Cedron, and all at once, Peter stopped and said, "Look, Paul, this is the very spot where Jesus wrestled, and where He suffered and sweat great drops of blood. There is the very spot where John and James fell asleep, right there. And right here is the very spot where I fell asleep. I don't think I would have denied Him if I hadn't gone to sleep, but I was overcome. I remember the last thing I heard Him say before I fell asleep was, 'Father, let this cup pass from me if it is Your will.' And when I awoke, an angel stood right there where you are standing, talking to Him, and I saw great drops of blood come from His pores and trickle down His cheeks. It wasn't long before Judas came to betray Him. I heard Him say to Judas so kindly, 'Do you betray the Master with a kiss?' And then they bound Him and led Him away. That night when He was on trial, I denied Him."

The next day Peter turned again to Paul and said, "Wouldn't you like to take another walk today?" Paul said he would. That day they went to Calvary, and when they got on the hill, Peter said, "Here, Paul, this is the very spot where Jesus died for you and me. See that hole right there? That is where His cross stood. The believing thief hung there and the unbelieving thief there on the other side. Mary Magdalene and Mary, His mother, stood there, and I stood away on the outskirts of the crowd. The night before, when I denied Him, He looked at me so lovingly that it broke my heart, and I couldn't bear to get near enough to see Him. That was the darkest hour of my life. I hoped that God would intercede and take Him from the cross. I kept listening and I thought I would hear His voice."

Andrew Bonar pictured the whole scene, how they drove the spear into His side and put the crown of thorns on His brow, and all else that took place. Bonar continued, saying that the next day Peter turned to Paul again and asked him if he would like to take another walk. Again, Paul said he would. Again, they passed down the streets of Jerusalem, over the brook Cedron, over the Mount of Olives, up to Bethphage, and over onto the hill near Bethany. All at once Peter stopped and said, "Here, Paul, this is the last place where I ever saw Him. I never heard Jesus speak so sweetly as He did that day. It was right here where He delivered His last message to us, and all at once, I noticed that His feet didn't touch the ground. He arose and went up. All at once, there came a cloud and it received Him out of our sight. I stood right here gazing up into the heavens, hoping that I might see Him again and hear Him speak. And two men dressed in white dropped down by our sides and stood there and said, '*Men of Galilee, why do you stand looking into the sky? This Jesus, who has been taken up from you into heaven, will come in just the same way as you have watched Him go into heaven*' (Acts 1:11).

My friends, I want to ask you this question: Do you believe that picture is overdrawn? Do you believe Peter had Paul as his guest and didn't take him to Gethsemane, didn't take him to Calvary and to the Mount of Olives? I myself spent eight days in Jerusalem, and every morning I wanted to slip down into the garden where my Lord sweat great drops of blood. Every day I climbed the Mount of Olives and looked up into the blue sky where Jesus went to His Father. I have no doubt that Peter took Paul out on those three walks. If there had been a man that could have taken me to the very spot where the Master sweat those great drops of blood, do you think I wouldn't have asked him to take me there? If he could have told me where I could find the spot where my Master's feet last touched this sin-cursed earth and was taken up, do you think I wouldn't have had him show it to me?

I know there is a class of people who say that kind of practical preaching won't do in this country. "People want something grandiose." Well, there is no doubt that there are some who want to hear fancy, flowery sermons, but they forget them inside of twenty-four hours.

It a good thing for a minister to have the reputation of feeding his people. A man once made an artificial bee, which was so like a real bee that he challenged another man to tell the difference. It buzzed just like the live bee, and it looked the same. The other man said, "You put an artificial bee and a real bee down there, and I will tell you the difference pretty quickly." He then put a drop of honey on the ground and the live bee went for the honey.

It is just so with us. There are a lot of people who profess to be Christians, but they are artificial and they don't know when you give them honey. The real bees go for honey every time. People can get along without your theories and opinions. *Thus saith the Lord* – that is what we need. Give them the Word of God.

Chapter 8

Take Time and Study

Merely reading the Bible is not what God wants. Again and again we are exhorted to "search."

> *Now these were more noble-minded than those in Thessalonica, for they received the word with great eagerness, examining the Scriptures daily to see whether these things were so.* (Acts 17:11)

> *They read from the book, from the law of God, translating to give the sense so that they understood the reading.* (Nehemiah 8:8)

We must study the Bible thoroughly and hunt through it, as it were, for some great truth. If a friend were to see me searching around a building and were to come up and say, "Moody, what are you looking for? Have you lost something?" and I answered, "No, I haven't lost anything. I'm not looking for anything in particular,"

I suppose he would just leave me alone, and think me very foolish. But if I were to say, "Yes, I have lost a dollar," then I might expect him to help me find it. Read the Bible, my friends, as if you were seeking for something of value. It is a good deal better to take a single chapter and spend a week on it than to read the Bible at random for a week.

> *My son, if you will receive my words and trea-*
> *sure my commandments within you, make*
> *your ear attentive to wisdom, incline your*
> *heart to understanding; For if you cry for dis-*
> *cernment, lift your voice for understanding;*
> *If you seek her as silver and search for her as*
> *for hidden treasures; Then you will discern the*
> *fear of the LORD and discover the knowledge*
> *of God.* (Proverbs 2:1-5)

There was a time when I used to read a certain number of chapters a day, and if I did not get through my usual quantity, I thought I was getting cold and backsliding. But if a man had asked me two hours later what I had read, I could not tell him; I had forgotten nearly all of it. When I was a boy, one thing I used to do was to hoe corn on a farm. I used to hoe it so poorly in order to get over so much ground, though, that at night I had to put a stick in the ground so I knew the next morning where I had left off. That was somewhat the same as reading through a certain number of chapters every day. I read to meet my requirements, and not to grow closer to God.

A man will say, "Wife, did I read that chapter?"

"Well," says she, "I don't remember."

Neither of them can remember, and so he might then read the same chapter over and over again; and they call that "studying the Bible." I do not think there is a book in the world we neglect so much as the Bible.

This is how many group Bible studies are today. Men and women sit around and read a little book, and then say, "What do you think?" Then they ask the next person, "What do you think?" At the end, you know what everyone thinks, but no one knows what God says. Too often we start and end with our opinions instead of the Word of God.

Now, when you read the Bible at family worship or for private devotions, look for suitable passages. What would you think of a minister who went into the pulpit on Sunday and opened the Bible at random and began to read? Yet this is what most men do at family prayers. They might as well go into a drugstore and swallow the first medicine their eye happens to see. Children would take more interest in family prayers if the father would take time to search for some passage to suit a specific need. For instance, if any member of the family is about to travel, read Psalm 121. In time of trouble, read Psalm 91. When the terrible accident happened to the Spree as we were crossing the Atlantic in November 1892, and when none on board ship expected to live to see the light of another sun, we held a prayer meeting, at which I read Psalm 107:23-31:

> *Those who go down to the sea in ships, who*
> *do business on great waters; They have seen*

the works of the LORD, and His wonders
in the deep. For He spoke and raised up a
stormy wind, which lifted up the waves of the
sea. They rose up to the heavens, they went
down to the depths; Their soul melted away
in their misery. They reeled and staggered like
a drunken man, and were at their wits' end.
Then they cried to the LORD in their trouble,
and He brought them out of their distresses.
He caused the storm to be still, so that the
waves of the sea were hushed. Then they were
glad because they were quiet, so He guided
them to their desired haven. Let them give
thanks to the LORD for His lovingkindness,
and for His wonders to the sons of men!

A lady came to me afterwards and accused me of making that passage up to suit the occasion. She did not know it was in the Bible. We need to get to know the Bible, and use it!

There are some questions that will help us get some good out of every verse and passage of Scripture. They may be used in family worship, in studying the Sunday school lesson, for prayer meeting, or in private reading. It would be a good thing if questions like these were written in the front of every Bible:

1. What people have I read about, and what have I learned about them?

2. What places have I read about, and what have I learned about them? If the place is

not mentioned, can I find out where it is? Do I know its position on the map?

3. Does the passage refer to any particular time in the history of the children of Israel, or of some leading character?

4. Can I tell from memory what I have just been reading?

5. Are there any parallel passages or texts that throw light on this passage?

6. Have I read anything about God the Father, or about Jesus Christ, or about the Holy Spirit?

7. What have I read about myself, about man's sinful nature, or about the spiritual new nature?

8. Is there any duty for me to observe? Any example to follow? Any promise to lay hold of? Any exhortation for my guidance? Any prayer that I may pray?

9. How is this Scripture profitable for doctrine, for reproof, for correction, and for instruction in righteousness?

10. Does the passage of Scripture contain the gospel?

11. Is there a main verse of the chapter or passage? Can I repeat it from memory?

Chapter 9

Learn and Use the Bible

Someone has said that there are four things necessary in studying the Bible: admit, submit, commit, and transmit. First, admit its truth. Second, submit to its teachings. Third, commit it to memory. Fourth, transmit it. If the Christian life is a good thing for you, pass it on to someone else.

I want to tell you how I study the Bible. Every man cannot fight in Saul's armor, and perhaps you cannot follow my methods. Still, I may be able to throw out some suggestions that will help you. Spurgeon used to prepare his sermon for Sunday morning on Saturday night. If I tried that, I would fail.

The quicker you learn to feed yourself, the better. I pity down deep in my heart any men or women who have been attending some church or chapel for five, ten, or twenty years, and yet have not learned to feed themselves spiritually. They rely on the pastor or

Sunday school teacher, but they do not feed themselves on the Word of God.

You know it is always regarded as a great event in the family when a child can feed himself. A child might be sitting in a high chair, and at first, perhaps he uses the spoon upside down, but soon he uses it the right way, and mother or sister claps her hands and says, "Look! Baby's feeding himself!" Well, what we need as Christians is to be able to feed ourselves. There are many who sit helpless and weak, with open mouths, hungry for spiritual things, and the minister has to try to feed them, while the Bible is a feast prepared from which they never eat on their own. Not all ministers feed the people much either, so we need to be sure to feed ourselves every day.

There are many who have been Christians for twenty years who still rely on being fed only at church. If they happen to have a pastor who feeds them, they can get by; but if they have a pastor who gives sermons instead of messages from God, they are not fed at all. This is one way to know if you are a true child of God – whether you love and feed upon the Word of God on your own. If you go out to your garden and throw down some sawdust, the birds will not take any notice; but if you throw down some crumbs, they will soon sweep down and pick them up. In the same way, the true child of God can tell the difference between spiritual sawdust and bread. Are you being changed by God's Word, or are you only attending a church service? Many so-called Christians are living on the world's sawdust instead of being nourished by the Bread that comes down from heaven. Nothing can satisfy the longings of the soul but the Word of the living God.

> *Your words were found and I ate them, and Your words became for me a joy and the delight of my heart.* (Jeremiah 15:16)

The best law for Bible study is the law of perseverance. The psalmist says, *I cling to Your testimonies* (Psalm 119:31). Diligence and discipline in studying the Word will allow it to grow within and show without. Some people are like express trains; they skim along so quickly that they see nothing.

I met a lawyer in Chicago who told me he had spent two years studying one subject. He was trying to overturn a will. He made it his business to read everything on wills he could get. Then he went into court and he talked for two days about that will; he could not talk about anything else but wills. That is the way with the Bible – study it and study it, one subject at a time, until you become filled with it.

Read the Bible itself; do not spend all your time on commentaries and helps. If a man spent all his time reading up on the chemical constituents of bread and milk, he would soon starve. Devotional books can be helpful too, but do not think that a devotional book can replace your time in the Word of God.

There are three books which I think every Christian ought to possess. The first, of course, is the Bible. I believe in getting a good Bible with good plain print. I have not much love for those little Bibles that you have to hold right under your nose in order to read the print; and if the church happens to be a little dark, you cannot see the print, but it becomes a mere jumble of words. Yes, but someone will say you cannot carry a big Bible in your pocket. Very well, then, carry it under your arm; and if you have to walk five miles, you will just be preaching a sermon five miles long. I know a man who was convicted just by seeing another man carrying his Bible under his arm. You are not ashamed to carry other books, so why would you be ashamed to be seen carrying a Bible? If you get a good Bible, you are likely to take better care of it. Suppose you pay fifty dollars for a good Bible; the older you grow, the more precious it will become to you. Be sure you do not get one so good that you will be afraid to mark it. I don't like gilt-edged Bibles that look as if they had never been used.

Next, I would advise you to get a concordance. I was a Christian about five years before I ever heard of a concordance. When I was newly saved, I talked with a skeptic in Boston. I didn't know much about the Bible, but I tried to defend the Bible and Christianity. He quoted the Bible incorrectly, and I told him that what he said was not in the Bible. I hunted for days and days. If I had had a concordance, I could have found it at once. It is a good thing for ministers once in awhile to tell the people about a good book. You can find any portion or any verse in the Bible by just turning to a concordance.

Thirdly, get a topical Bible. These three books will help you to study the Word of God with profit. If you do not have them, get them at once; every Christian ought to have them.[3]

These books are good to study from and to help you learn, but I think teachers should not rely on them in class. They should use the Bible, and all of it. Sunday school teachers are making a big mistake if they don't take the whole Bible into their Sunday school classes. I don't care how young children are; let them understand it is one book, that there are not two books. The Old Testament and the New are all one. Don't let them think that the Old Testament doesn't come to us with the same authority as the New. It is a great thing for a boy or girl to know how to handle the Bible. What is an army good for if the soldiers don't know how to handle their weapons? I speak very strongly on this, because I know some Sunday schools that don't have a single Bible in them. They have question books. There are questions and the answers are given below, so that you don't need to study your lesson. They are splendid things for lazy teachers to bring along into their classes.

I have seen a Sunday school teacher ask a student questions that went something like this:

"John, who was the first man?"

"Methuselah."

"No, I don't think so; let me see. No, it is not Methuselah. Can you guess again?"

"Elijah."

"No."

"Adam."

---

3   In this technological age, there are many electronic means to access these resources and study the Bible. One good way is with a free software program like e-sword (*www.e-sword.net*).

"That's right, my son; you must have studied your lesson hard."

Now, I would like to know what a boy is going to do with that kind of a teacher or with that kind of teaching. That kind of teaching is worthless and brings no result. I don't condemn helps. I believe in availing yourself of all the light you can get. What I want you to do when you come into your classes is to come prepared to explain the lesson without the use of a concordance. Bring the Word of God with you; bring the old Book.

You will sometimes find families where there is a family Bible, but the mother is so afraid that the children will tear it that she keeps it in the spare room, and once in a great while the children are allowed to look at it. The thing that interests them most is the family record – when John was born, when father and mother were married.

When I first came up to Boston from the country, I went to a Bible class where there were a few Harvard students. They handed me a Bible and told me the lesson was in John. I hunted all through the Old Testament for John, but couldn't find it. I saw the fellows looking at one another, saying, "Ah, a new kid from the country." Now, you know that is just the time when you don't want to be considered ignorant. The teacher saw my embarrassment and handed me his Bible, and I put my thumb in the place and held on. I didn't lose my place. I said then that if I ever got out of that scrape, I would never be caught there again.

Why is it that so many young people from eighteen to twenty cannot be brought into a Bible class? Because they don't want to show their ignorance. Many of our youth learn to play at church, but not to pray. They are taught to be happy, but not to be holy. There is no place in the world that is so fascinating as a live Bible class. I believe that we are to blame that they have been brought up in Sunday school with nice lessons but without knowing their Bibles. The result is that the children are growing up knowing what they are told, but not knowing what the Bible says. They don't know where Matthew is, they don't know where the epistle to the Ephesians is, they don't know where to find Hebrews or any of the different books of the Bible. They ought to be taught how to handle the whole Bible, and it can be done by Sunday school teachers taking the Bible into the class and going right at it. You can get a Bible in this country for almost a song now. Sunday schools are not so poor that they cannot get Bibles. Sunday school quarterlies are all right in their places, as helps in studying the lesson, but if they are going to sweep the Bibles out of our Sunday schools, I think we had better sweep *them* out.

Chapter 10

Try the Telescope Approach

There are two opposite ways to study the Bible. One way is to study it with a telescope, taking a grand sweep of a whole book and trying to find out God's plan in it. The other way is to study it with a microscope, taking up a verse at a time, dissecting and analyzing it. For example, Genesis is the seed plant of the whole Bible; it tells us of life, death, and resurrection. It involves all the rest of the Bible.

Here is one way to look at the Bible with a telescope, seeing the whole forest at once. An Englishman once remarked to me, "Mr. Moody, did you ever notice that the book of Job is the key to the whole Bible? If you understand Job, you will understand the entire Bible!"

"No," I said. "Why do you say that – 'Job is the key to the whole Bible'? How do you make that out?"

He said, "I divide Job into seven sections. The first section is *A perfect man untried*. That is what God said about Job; that is Adam in Eden. He was perfect when

God put him there. The second section is *Tried by adversity*. Job fell, as Adam fell in Eden. The third section is *The wisdom of the world*. The world tried to restore Job; the three wise men, Eliphaz, Bildad, and Zophar, came to help him. That was the wisdom of the world centered in those three men. You cannot find any such eloquent language or wisdom anywhere, in any part of the world, as those three men displayed, but they did not know anything about grace, and could not, therefore, help Job."

That is just what men are trying to do, and the result is that they fail. The wisdom of man never made man any better. These three men did not help Job; they made him more unhappy.

> *I have heard many such things; Sorry comforters are you all.* (Job 16:2)

The Englishman continued to explain his seven parts of Job to me. "Then in the fourth place," said he, "in comes *the arbiter or judge*; that is Christ. In the fifth place, *God speaks*; and in the sixth, *Job learns his lesson*. And then down came Job flat on the dunghill. The seventh section is this, that *God restores him*." Thank God, it is so with us, and our last state is better than our first.

> *I have heard of You by the hearing of the ear; But now my eye sees You; Therefore I retract, and I repent in dust and ashes.* (Job 42:5-6)

> *The LORD blessed the latter days of Job more than his beginning; and he had 14,000 sheep and 6,000 camels and 1,000 yoke of oxen and 1,000 female donkeys. He had seven sons and three daughters.* (Job 42:12-13)

A friend of mine said to me, "Look here, Moody. God gave Job double of everything." God had taken Job's children to heaven, and He gave Job ten more. So Job had ten children in heaven and ten on earth – a good-sized family. So when our children are taken from us, they are not lost to us, but merely gone before us.

Now, let's take that telescope approach through the four Gospels, beginning with Matthew. Men sometimes tell me when I go into a town, "Be sure and get such a man on your committee, for he has nothing to do and he will have plenty of time."

I say, "No, thank you. I do not want any man that has nothing to do." Christ found Matthew sitting at the receipt of customs. The Lord took someone He found at work and he went right on working. We do not know much about what he did, except that he wrote this gospel; but what a book! Where Matthew came from we do not know, and where he went we do not know. His old name, Levi, dropped with his old life.

Matthew writes about the Messiah of the Jews and the Savior of the world. His gospel contains the best account of the life of Christ. You notice that it is the last message of God to the Jewish nation.

Matthew does not speak of Christ's ascension, but leaves Him on earth.

Mark gives His resurrection and ascension.

Luke gives His resurrection, ascension, and the promise of a Comforter.

John goes a step further and says that Jesus is coming back.

There are more quotations from the Old Testament in

Matthew than in any of the other Gospels. I think there are about a hundred. Matthew was trying to convince the Jews that Jesus was the son of David, the rightful king. He talked a good deal about the kingdom, its mysteries, the example of the kingdom, healing the sick, the principles of the kingdom as set forth in the Sermon on the Mount, and the rejection of the King. When anyone takes a kingdom, he lays down the principles upon which he is going to rule.

Now, let me call your attention to five great sermons in the gospel of Matthew. In these, you have a good sweep of the whole book:

1. The Sermon on the Mount. See how many things lying all around Him He brings into His sermon: salt, light, candle, coat, rain, closet, moth, rust, thieves, eye, fowls, lilies, grass, dogs, bread, fish, gate, grapes, thorns, figs, thistles, rock, and more.

Someone, in traveling through Israel, said that he did not think there was a solitary thing there that Christ did not use as an illustration. So many people these days are afraid to use common things, but don't you think it is better to use things that people can understand than to talk so that people cannot understand you? Now, a woman can easily understand a candle, and a man can easily understand a rock, especially in a rocky country like Israel. Christ used common things as illustrations and spoke so that everyone could understand Him.

Christ did not have a reporter to go around with Him to write out and print His sermons, and yet the people remembered them. Never mind about fancy sentences and elegant words, but give your attention to making your sermons clear so that they stick. Use bait that your hearers will like. Some preachers spend more time trying to make nice outlines than they do seeking God.

The law was given on a mountain, and here Christ lays down His principles on a mountain. The law of Moses applies to the outward acts, but this sermon applies to the inward life. As the sun is brighter than a candle, so the Sermon on the Mount is brighter than the law of Moses. It tells us what kind of Christians we ought to be: lights in the world and the salt of the earth, silent in our actions, but great in effect.

I say unto you occurs thirteen times in this sermon.

2. The second great sermon in Matthew was delivered to the twelve disciples in the tenth chapter. You find simple sayings in this sermon that are often quoted, such as "Shake the dust off your feet against them," and "Freely you have received, freely give."

3. The open-air sermon, found in Matthew 13. This sermon contains nine parables. It is like a string of pearls. You want the best kind of preaching on the street? You have to put what you say in a bright, crisp way if you expect people to listen.

You must learn to think on your feet. There was a young man preaching on the streets in London when an infidel came up and said, "The man who invented gas lights did more for the world than Jesus Christ." The young man could not answer him and the crowd had the laugh on him. But another man got up and said,

"Of course the man has a right to his opinion, and I suppose if he was dying he would send for the gas fitter, but I think I would send for a minister and have him read the fourteenth chapter of John," and he turned the laugh back on the man.

4. The sermon of woes is the fourth great sermon in Matthew, and it is found in chapter 23. This is Christ's last appeal to the Jewish nation. Compare these eight woes with the nine beatitudes found in Matthew 5:3-12. The end of this sermon on woes is the most heartbreaking utterance in the whole ministry of Christ: *Behold, your house is being left to you desolate* (Matthew 23:38). Up to that time, it had been *My Father's* house, or *My* house, but now it is *your* house. It was not long until the Roman leader Titus came and leveled the temple to the ground. Abraham never loved Isaac more than Jesus loved the Jewish nation. It was hard for Abraham to give up Isaac, but harder for the Son of God to give up Jerusalem.

5. Jesus' fifth great sermon in Matthew was preached to His disciples. You can read it in Matthew chapter 24. How little did they understand Him! When His heart was breaking with sorrow, they drew His attention to the buildings of the temple.

In Matthew's gospel, there is not a thing in hell, heaven, earth, sea, air, or grave that does not testify of Christ as the Son of God. Devils cried out, fish entered the nets under His influence, wind and wave obeyed Him.

Summary: Nine beatitudes, eight woes, nine consecutive parables, ten consecutive miracles, five continuous sermons, and four prophecies of His death.

As we move on to the gospel of Mark, notice that the four Gospels are independent of each other; none was copied from the other. Each is the complement of the rest, and we get four views of Christ, like the four sides of a house. Matthew writes for Jews. Mark writes for Romans. Luke writes for Gentile converts.

You don't find any long sermons in Mark. The Romans were quick and active, and Mark had to condense things in order to catch them. You'll find words like *forthwith*, *straightway*, and *immediately* occurring thirty-two times in this gospel. Every chapter but the first, seventh, eighth, ninth, and fourteenth begins with *And*, as if there was no pause in Christ's ministry.

Luke tells us that Christ received little children, but Mark says He took them up in His arms. That makes it sweeter to you, doesn't it?

Perhaps the high-water mark is the fifth chapter. Here we find three very bad cases – devils, disease, and death – beyond the reach of man, cured by Christ. The first man was possessed with devils. The people could not bind or chain or tame him. I suppose many men and women had been scared by that man. People are afraid of a graveyard even in daylight, but think of a live man being in the tombs and possessed with devils! He said, *What business do we have with each other, Jesus, Son of the Most High God? I implore You by God, do not torment me* (Mark 5:7). But Jesus had come to do him good.

Next is the woman with the issue of blood (Mark 5:25-34). If she had been living today, I suppose she would have tried every medicine in the market. We would have declared her a hopeless case and sent her to the hospital. Someone has said, "There was more medicine in the hem of His garment than in all the drugstores in Israel." She just touched Him and was made whole. Hundreds of others touched Him, but they did not get anything. Can you tell the difference between the touch of faith and the ordinary touch of the crowd?

Thirdly, Jairus's daughter raised from the dead (Mark 5:22-24, 35-43). You see the manifestation of Jesus' power increasing, for when He arrived, the child was dead, and He brought her to life. I do not doubt but that way back in the secret councils of eternity, it was appointed that He should be there just at that time. I remember once being called to preach a funeral sermon, and I looked through the four Gospels to find one of Christ's funeral sermons; but do you know, He never preached one? He broke up every funeral He ever attended. The dead came to life when they heard His voice.

We now come to Luke's gospel. You notice his name does not occur in this book or in Acts. You will find Luke's name used three times: in Colossians, 2 Timothy, and Philemon. He keeps himself in the background. I meet numbers of Christian workers who are ruined by getting attention. We do not even know for certain whether Luke was a Jew or a Gentile.

The first we see of Luke is in Acts 16:10: *When he had seen the vision, immediately we sought to go into Macedonia, concluding that God had called us to preach the gospel to them.* He did not claim to be an eyewitness to Christ's ministry, nor did he claim to be one of the seventy (Luke 10). Some think he was, but he does not claim it. It is supposed that his gospel was from Paul's preaching, the same as Mark's was from Peter's. It is also called the Gospel of the Gentiles, and is supposed to have been written when Paul was in Rome, about twenty-seven years after Christ. One-third of this gospel is left out of the other Gospels. Luke opens with a note of praise: *You will have joy and gladness, and many will rejoice at his birth* (Luke 1:14). It closes the same way: *And they, after worshipping Him, returned to Jerusalem with great joy, and were continually in the temple praising God* (Luke 24:52-53).

Canon Frederic Farrar has pointed out that we have a sevenfold gospel in Luke:

1. It is a gospel of praise and song. We find here the songs of Zacharias, Elizabeth, Mary, Simeon, the angels, and others.

Read what the Rev. James Caughey wrote about Simeon in his book *Helps to a Life of Holiness and Usefulness*:

> What Simeon wanted was to see the Lord's Christ. Unbelief would suggest to him, "Simeon, you are an old man; your day is almost ended; the snow of age is upon your head; your eyes are growing dim, your brow is wrinkled, your limbs totter, and death cannot be at a great distance, and where are the signs of his coming? You

are resting, Simeon, on a phantom of the imagination – it is all a delusion."

"No," replies Simeon, "I shall not see death till I have seen the Lord's Christ. Yes, I shall see him before I die."

But unbelief would again suggest, "Remember, Simeon, many holy men have desired to see the Lord's Christ, but have died without the sight."

"Yes," says Simeon, "I shall see the Lord's Christ."

I imagine I see Simeon walking out on a fine morning along one of the lovely valleys of Israel, meditating on the great subject that filled his mind. He is met by one of his friends, who says, "Peace be with you. Have you heard the strange news?"

"What news?" asks Simeon.

"Do you know Zacharias the priest?"

"Yes, very well."

"According to the custom of the priest's office, his lot was to burn incense in the temple of the Lord, and the whole multitude of the people were praying outside. It was the time of incense, and there appeared unto him an angel standing on the right side of the altar of incense, and told him that he would have a son, who would be called John. The angel said that the son of Zacharias would be great in the sight of the Lord; he should neither drink wine nor strong drink, and he would be filled with the Holy Spirit from his infancy. He would go before the

Messiah in the spirit and power of Elijah, to turn many of the people of Israel to the Lord, and make ready a people prepared for the Lord. The angel was Gabriel, who stands in the presence of God. Because Zacharias did not believe the angel, he was struck mute."

"Ah!" says Simeon. "That is an exact fulfillment of the prophecy of Malachi 4:5-6: *Behold, I am going to send you Elijah the prophet before the coming of the great and terrible day of the LORD. He will restore the hearts of the fathers to their children and the hearts of the children to their fathers, so that I will not come and smite the land with a curse.* This is the messenger of the Lord, to prepare the way; this is the forerunner; this is the morning star; the day's dawn is not far off; the great Messiah is on His way. He is near. I will not see death till I have seen the Lord's Christ. Hallelujah! The Lord will suddenly come to His temple" (Malachi 3:1).

Simeon pondered these things in his heart, and time rolled on. I imagine I see Simeon again on his morning meditative walk. He is again accosted by one of his neighbors, who says, "Well, Simeon, have you heard the news?"

"What news?"

"A company of shepherds on the plains of Bethlehem was watching their flocks; it was the still hour of night, and the mantle of darkness covered the world. A bright light shone around the shepherds, a light above the brightness of the midday sun. They looked up, and just above them appeared an angel glowing in all the lovely hues of heaven. The shepherds became greatly terrified, and the angel said to them, *Do not be afraid; for behold,*

I bring you good news of great joy which will be for all the people (Luke 2:10).

"This is the Lord's Christ. I will not see death until I have seen the Lord's Christ." Then Simeon probably says to himself, "They will bring Him to the temple to circumcise Him." Away goes Simeon, morning after morning, to see if he can get a glimpse of Jesus.

Perhaps unbelief suggests to Simeon, "You had better stay at home this wet morning. You have been there so many mornings and have not seen Him; you can miss this one day."

"No," says the Spirit, "you must go to the temple." Away goes Simeon to the temple. He would no doubt select a good post of observation. Look at him there, leaning his back against one of the pillars of the temple; how intently he watches the door! He sees one mother after another bringing her infant to the temple to be circumcised. He surveys the face of every child.

"No," says he, as his eye scans the countenance, "that is not Him, and that is not Him"; but at length he sees the virgin Mary appear, and the Holy Spirit told him that this baby was the long-expected Savior. He grasps the child in his arms and presses Him to his heart, and exclaims, *"Now Lord, You are releasing Your bond-servant to depart in peace, according to Your word; For my eyes have seen Your salvation"* (Luke 2:29-30).

2. Luke is a gospel of thanksgiving. They glorified God when Jesus healed the widow's son at Nain, when the blind man received sight, etc.

3. It is a gospel of prayer. We learn that Christ prayed when He was baptized, and nearly every great event in His ministry was preceded by prayer. If you want to hear from heaven, you must seek God in earnest prayer. There are two parables about prayer: the friend at midnight (Luke 11:5-8) and the unjust judge (Luke 18:1-8).

4. Here is another thing that is made prominent, namely, the gospel of womanhood. Luke alone records many loving things Christ did for women. The richest jewel in Christ's crown was what He did for women. A man once tried to tell me that Muhammad had done more for women than Christ had. I told him that if he had ever been in Islamic countries, he would be ashamed of himself for making such a remark.

5. This is the gospel of the poor and humble. When I speak to a rough crowd on the street, I generally teach from Luke. Here are the shepherds, the peasants, and the incident of the rich man and Lazarus. This gospel tells us *he found the place where it was written, The Spirit of the Lord GOD is upon me, because the LORD has anointed me to bring good news to the afflicted* (Isaiah 61:1). It is a dark day for a church when they do not want the common people. George Whitefield labored among the miners, and John Wesley among the common people. If you want the poor, let it be known that you want them to come.

6. Luke is a gospel to the lost. The woman with the seven devils and the thief on the cross illustrate this, as do the parables of the lost sheep, the lost piece of silver, and the lost son.

7. It is a gospel of tolerance.

Luke shows us how Jesus won the lost. *He who is wise wins souls* (Proverbs 11:30). Do you want to win people to Jesus? Do not try to tear down their prejudices before you begin to lead them to the truth. Some people think they have to tear down the scaffolding before they begin work on the building. An old minister once invited a young brother to preach for him. The latter scolded the people, and when he got home, he asked the old minister how he had done. The old minister said he had an old cow, and when he wanted a good supply of milk, he fed the cow; he did not scold her.

Christ reached the publicans because nearly everything He said about them was in their favor. Look at the parable of the Pharisee and the publican (Luke 18:9-14). Christ said the publican went down to his house justified rather than that proud Pharisee.

How did He reach the Samaritans? Take the parable of the ten lepers. Only one returned to thank Him for the healing, and that was a Samaritan. Then there is the parable of the good Samaritan. It has done more to stir people up to philanthropy and kindness to the poor than anything else that has been said on this earth for six thousand years.

If you want to reach people who do not agree with you, do not take a club to knock them down and then try to pick them up. When Jesus Christ dealt with the erring and the sinners, He was as tender with them as a mother is with her sick child.

Chapter 11

From the Telescope to the Microscope

The fourth gospel was written by John. John is thought to be the youngest disciple and the first one to follow Christ. He is called the bosom companion of Christ. Someone was complaining that Jesus was being partial. I have no doubt that Christ loved John more than the others, but perhaps it was because John loved Him most. I think John got into the inner circle, and we can get in too if we will. Christ keeps the door open and we can just go right in. You notice that nearly all of John's gospel is new from what is in the other three gospels. All of the eight months Christ spent in Judea are recorded here.

Matthew begins with Abraham, Mark with Malachi, and Luke with John the Baptist, but John begins with God Himself. Matthew sets forth Christ as the Jews' Messiah, Mark shows Him as the active worker, and

Luke writes about Jesus as a man, while John portrays Him as a personal Savior.

John presents Him as coming from the bosom of the Father. The central thought in this gospel is proving the divinity of Christ. If I wanted to prove to someone that Jesus Christ was divine, I would take him directly to this gospel. The word *repent* does not occur once, but the word *believe* occurs eighty-five times. The controversy that the Jews raised about the divinity of Christ was not yet settled, and before John went away, he took his pen and wrote down these things to settle it.

John gives us a sevenfold witness to the divinity of Christ:

1. Testimony of the Father: *The Father who sent Me testifies about Me* (John 8:18).

2. Testimony of the Son: *Jesus answered and said to them, Even if I testify about Myself, My testimony is true, for I know where I came from and where I am going; but you do not know where I come from or where I am going* (John 8:14).

3. Testimony of Christ's works: *If I do not do the works of My Father, do not believe Me; but if I do them, though you do not believe Me, believe the works, so that you may know and understand that the Father is in Me, and I in the Father* (John 10:37-38).

No man can make me believe that Jesus Christ was a bad man, because He brought forth good fruit. How anyone can doubt that He was the Son of God after twenty centuries of testing is a mystery to me.

4. Testimony of the Scriptures: *For if you believed Moses, you would believe Me, for he wrote about Me* (John 5:46).

5. Testimony of John the Baptist: *I myself have seen, and have testified that this is the Son of God* (John 1:34).

6. Testimony of the disciples: *And you will testify also, because you have been with Me from the beginning* (John 15:27).

7. Testimony of the Holy Spirit: *When the Helper comes, whom I will send to you from the Father, that is the Spirit of truth who proceeds from the Father, He will testify about Me* (John 15:26).

Of course, there are many other verses that show His divinity, but I think these are enough to prove it to anyone. If I went into court and had seven witnesses who could not be broken down, I think I would have a good case.

Notice the *I am* statements of Christ from the gospel of John:

- *I am from above.* (John 8:23)

- *I am not of this world.* (John 8:23)

- *I am not of the world.* (John 17:16)

- *Before Abraham was born, I AM.* (John 8:58)

- *I AM the bread of life.* (John 6:35)

- *I AM the light of the world.* (John 8:12)

- *I AM the door.* (John 10:9)

- *I AM the good shepherd.* (John 10:11, 14)

- *I AM the way, and the truth, and the life* (John 14:6). Pilate asked what truth was, and there it was, standing right before him.

- *I AM the resurrection and the life.* (John 11:25)

In the gospel of John, we find eight gifts for the believer: the bread of life, the water of life, eternal life, the Holy Spirit, love, joy, peace, and His words.

Now that we have looked at the Gospels through the telescope, let's take a look at the book of Acts. A good lesson to study is how all through the book of Acts, defeat was turned to victory. When the early Christians were persecuted, they went everywhere preaching the Word. That was a victory, and so on all through the book.

Luke's gospel tells of Christ in the body, while Acts tells of Christ in the church. In Luke, we read of what Christ did in His humiliation, and in Acts, what He did in His exaltation. With most men, their work stops at their death, but with Christ, it had only begun. *Greater works than these he will do; because I go to the Father* (John 14:12). We call this book the Acts of the Apostles, but it is really the Acts of the Church (Christ's body).

You will find the key to the book in Acts 1:8: *But you*

will receive power when the Holy Spirit has come upon you; and you shall be My witnesses both in Jerusalem, and in all Judea and Samaria, and even to the remotest part of the earth.

We would not have seen the struggles of that infant church if it had not been for Luke. We would not have known much about Paul either, if it had not been for Luke.

There were four rivers flowing out of Eden (Genesis 2:10-14); here in Acts, we have the four Gospels flowing into one channel. I believe that the nearer we keep to the apostles' way of presenting the gospel, the more success we will have. Some want to reach the lost by imitating the world. It is far better to follow the example of the apostles.

There are ten great sermons in Acts, and I think if you get a good hold on these you will have a pretty good understanding of the book and how to preach. Five of the sermons were preached by Peter, one by Stephen, and four by Paul. The phrase *we are witnesses* runs through the entire book. Today, though, we say, "We are eloquent preachers." We seem to want to be above being simple witnesses.

1. Peter's sermon on the day of Pentecost (Acts 2). Someone said that it takes about three thousand sermons to convert one Jew, but here three thousand Jews were converted by one sermon. When Peter testified of Christ and bore witness that He had died and risen again, God honored it, and He will do the same with you.

Everyone who calls on the name of the Lord
will be saved. (Acts 2:21)

2. Peter preaches in Solomon's porch (Acts 3). It was a short sermon, but it did good work. They did not get there until three o'clock in the afternoon, and I believe the Jews could not arrest a man after sundown, and yet in that short space of time, five thousand were converted. What did he preach? Listen:

> *But you disowned the Holy and Righteous*
> *One and asked for a murderer to be granted*
> *to you, but put to death the Prince of life,*
> *the one whom God raised from the dead,*
> *a fact to which we are witnesses. Therefore*
> *repent and return, so that your sins may be*
> *wiped away, in order that times of refresh-*
> *ing may come from the presence of the Lord.*
> (Acts 3:14-15, 19)

3. Peter preaches to the high priests (Acts 4:1-12). They had arrested Peter and John and were demanding to know by what power they did what they did. Peter answered, *Let it be known to all of you and to all the people of Israel, that by the name of Jesus Christ the Nazarene, whom you crucified, whom God raised from the dead -by this name this man stands here before you in good health* (Acts 4:10). When John Bunyan, author of *The Pilgrim's Progress*, was told he would be released if he would not preach anymore, he said, "If you let me out, I will preach tomorrow."

> *And there is salvation in no one else; for there*
> *is no other name under heaven that has been*
> *given among men by which we must be saved.*
> (Acts 4:12)

4. Peter's testimony before the council (Acts 4:13-22). They commanded Peter and John not to preach in the name of Christ. I don't know what they would have done if they could not preach Christ. Some ministers today would have no trouble; they could get along very well without preaching Christ. About all the disciples knew was what they had learned in those three years with Jesus, hearing His sermons and seeing His miracles. They saw the things and knew they were so, and when the Holy Spirit came down upon them, they could not help but speak them. Do people see your life and hear your words and conclude that *Now as they observed the confidence of Peter and John and understood that they were uneducated and untrained men, they were amazed, and began to recognize them as having been with Jesus* (Acts 4:13)?

5. Stephen's sermon (Acts 7:2-53). Stephen preached the longest sermon in Acts. Dr. Bonar once said, "Did you ever notice that when the Jews accused Stephen of blasphemy against Moses' law, God lit up Stephen's face with the same glory that He had given to the face of Moses?"

An old Scotch church usher once warned his new minister: "You may preach as much as you like about the sins of Abraham, Isaac, and Jacob, but stick to their sins and don't come any nearer to ours if you want to stay here." Many church people don't mind condemning the sins of those outside the church, but they do not want to deal with the sins inside the church. Stephen began with the Jewish forefathers, but he came right down to the recent crucifixion, and he stirred them up.

> *You men who are stiff-necked and uncir-*
> *cumcised in heart and ears are always*
> *resisting the Holy Spirit; you are doing just*
> *as your fathers did. Now when they heard*
> *this, they were cut to the quick, and they*
> *began gnashing their teeth at him. They*
> *went on stoning Stephen as he called on*
> *the Lord and said, Lord Jesus, receive my*
> *spirit! Then falling on his knees, he cried out*
> *with a loud voice, Lord , do not hold this*
> *sin against them! Having said this, he fell*
> *asleep.* (Acts 7:51, 54, 59-60)

6. Peter's last sermon and the first sermon to the Gentiles (Acts 10:34-45). Notice the same gospel is preached to the Gentiles as to the Jews, and it produces the same results.

> *Of Him all the prophets bear witness that*
> *through His name everyone who believes in*
> *Him receives forgiveness of sins. While Peter*
> *was still speaking these words, the Holy Spirit*
> *fell upon all those who were listening to the*
> *message.* (Acts 10:43-44)

Now the leading character changes and Paul comes on the scene.

7. Paul's sermon at Antioch in Pisidia (Acts 13:16-41). An old acquaintance once said to me, "What are you preaching now? I hope you are not still harping on that old gospel." Yes, thank God, I am spreading the old gospel. If you want to get people to come hear you, lift up Christ. Jesus said, *And I, if I am lifted up from the earth, will draw all men to Myself* (John 12:32). Paul preached the gospel of Jesus Christ.

> *Therefore let it be known to you, brethren,*
> *that through Him forgiveness of sins is pro-*
> *claimed to you, and through Him everyone*
> *who believes is freed from all things, from*
> *which you could not be freed through the*
> *Law of Moses. Therefore take heed, so that*
> *the thing spoken of in the Prophets may not*
> *come upon you.* (Acts 13:38-40)

8. Paul's sermon to the Athenians (Acts 17:22-31). He got fruit at Athens by preaching the same old gospel to the philosophers.

> *Therefore having overlooked the times of*
> *ignorance, God is now declaring to men*
> *that all people everywhere should repent,*
> *because He has fixed a day in which He will*
> *judge the world in righteousness through*
> *a Man whom He has appointed, having*

*furnished proof to all men by raising Him
from the dead.* (Acts 17:30-31)

9. Paul's sermon, his testimony, at Jerusalem (Acts
22:1-21).

*Now why do you delay? Get up and be bap-
tized, and wash away your sins, calling on
His name.* (Acts 22:16)

10. Paul's defense before Agrippa (Acts 26:1-29). I think
this is the best sermon Paul ever preached. He preached
the same gospel before Agrippa and Festus that he
did down in Jerusalem. He preached everywhere the
mighty fact that God gave Christ as a ransom for sin,
that the whole world can be saved by trusting in Him.

*So, having obtained help from God, I stand
to this day testifying both to small and great,
stating nothing but what the Prophets and
Moses said was going to take place; that the
Christ was to suffer, and that by reason of
His resurrection from the dead He would be
the first to proclaim light both to the Jewish
people and to the Gentiles.* (Acts 26:22-23)

We have looked at the telescopic method in order to see
the big picture. Let me now briefly show what I mean
by the microscopic method. Take the first verse of
Psalm 52: *Why do you boast in evil, O mighty man? The
lovingkindness of God endures all day long.* This verse
naturally falls into two divisions: man on the one side,
and God on the other. Man – evil; God – mercy. Is any

particular man addressed? Yes, Doeg the Edomite, as the preface to the psalm suggests. You can find the historic reference of this verse and psalm in 1 Samuel 22:9. Now take a concordance or topical Bible and study the subject of boasting. What words mean the same thing as *boasting*? One synonym is *glorifying*. Is boasting always condemned? In what does Scripture forbid us to boast? In what are we exhorted to boast?

> *Thus says the LORD, Let not a wise man boast of his wisdom, and let not the mighty man boast of his might, let not a rich man boast of his riches; but let him who boasts boast of this, that he understands and knows Me, that I am the LORD who exercises lovingkindness, justice and righteousness on earth; for I delight in these things, declares the LORD.* (Jeremiah 9:23-24)

Treat the subject of evil in a similar manner. Then ask yourself if this boasting, this evil, is going to last always. No. *The triumphing of the wicked is short, and the joy of the hypocrite but for a moment* (Job 20:5). *I have seen a wicked, violent man spreading himself like a luxuriant tree in its native soil. Then he passed away, and lo, he was no more; I sought for him, but he could not be found* (Psalm 37:35-36).

The other half of Psalm 52:1, *The lovingkindness of God endures all day long,* suggests a study of mercy (or goodness) as an attribute of God. How is it manifested temporally and spiritually? What verses do we have about it? Is God's mercy conditional? Does God's mercy conflict with His justice? Now, since the goal of Bible study as well as of preaching is to save the lost, ask yourself if the gospel is contained in this text. Turn to Romans 2:4: *Or do you think lightly of the riches of His kindness and tolerance and patience, not knowing that the kindness of God leads you to repentance?* Here the verse leads directly to the subject of repentance, and you rise from the study of the verse ready at any time to preach a short sermon that may be the means of converting someone.

Chapter 12

Look and Learn; Read and Remember

I know some men who never sit down to read a book of the Bible until they have time to read the entire book at once. When they come to Leviticus or Numbers, or any of the other books, they read it all the way through at one sitting. They get the whole picture of the book, and then they begin to study it chapter by chapter. Dean Stanley used to read a book through three separate times: first for the story, second for the thought, and third for the literary style. It is a good thing to take one whole book at a time. How could you expect to understand a story or a scientific textbook if you read one chapter here and another there?

Dr. A. T. Pierson says, "Let the introduction cover five P's: place where written, person by whom written, people to whom written, purpose for which written, and period at which written."

It can be very beneficial to get the overall picture of a book of the Bible, and then to look at it more carefully. It can be good to grasp the leading points in the chapters. This method is illustrated by the following plan I tried to get the students at our Mount Hermon boys' school and the Northfield girls' school interested in. It provides a way of committing Scripture to memory so that one can call up a passage to meet the demand whenever it arises. I said to the students one morning at worship, "Tomorrow morning when I come, I will not read a portion of Scripture, but we will take the first chapter of the gospel of John and I want you to tell me from memory what you find in that chapter. We will each learn the verse in it that is most precious to us." We went through the whole book that way and committed a verse or two to memory out of each chapter.

Here are the main headings we found in the chapters:

Chapter 1. The call of the first five disciples.

It was about four o'clock in the afternoon when John stood and said, *Behold the Lamb of God* (John 1:29). Two of John's disciples then followed Jesus, and one of them, Andrew, went out and brought his brother, Simon. Then Jesus found Philip as he was starting out for Galilee, and Philip found Nathanael, the skeptical man. When he got sight of Christ, his skeptical ideas were all gone. Commit the following verses to memory:

> *He came to His own, and those who were*
> *His own did not receive Him. But as many*
> *as received Him, to them He gave the right*

*to become children of God, even to those
who believe in His name.* (John 1:11-12)

Key word: Receiving

Chapter 2. We had a good time in this chapter learning to obey.

Whatever He says to you, do it. (John 2:5)

Key word: Obedience

Chapter 3. This is a chapter on regeneration, or the new birth. It took us more than one day to get through this one. This chapter tells about a respectable, religious sinner and how Jesus dealt with him.

*For God so loved the world that he gave his
only begotten Son, that whoever believes in
him shall not perish, but have eternal life.*
(John 3:16)

Key word: Believing

Chapter 4. A disreputable sinner and how Jesus dealt with her. If we had been dealing with her, we would have told her what Jesus told Nicodemus, but He dealt with her differently, as her own individual person. She came for a pot of water, and thank God, she got a whole well full.

*God is spirit, and those who worship Him
must worship in spirit and truth.* (John 4:24)

Key word: Worshipping

Chapter 5. Divinity of Christ.

> *Truly, truly, I say to you, he who hears My word, and believes Him who sent Me, has eternal life, and does not come into judgment, but has passed out of death into life.* (John 5:24)

Key word: Healing

Chapter 6. We called this the *bread* chapter. If you want a good loaf of bread, get into this sixth chapter. You feed upon that bread and you will live forever.

> *I AM the living bread that came down out of heaven; if anyone eats of this bread, he will live forever; and the bread also which I will give for the life of the world is My flesh.* (John 6:51)

Key word: Eating

Chapter 7. The *water* chapter. You have here living water and Christ's invitation to every thirsty soul to come and drink.

> *If anyone is thirsty, let him come to Me and drink.* (John 7:37)

Key word: Drinking

Chapter 8. The *light* chapter. What is the use of having light if you have no eyes to see with? We need to get the sight found in the next chapter.

> *I AM the Light of the world; he who follows*

> *Me will not walk in the darkness, but will*
> *have the Light of life.* (John 8:12)

Key words: Walking in the light

Chapter 9. The *sight* chapter. There was a man born blind and Christ made him to see.

> *We must work the works of Him who sent*
> *Me as long as it is day; night is coming*
> *when no one can work.* (John 9:4)

Key word: Testifying

Chapter 10. Here you find the Good Shepherd.

> *I AM the good shepherd; the good shepherd*
> *lays down His life for the sheep.* (John 10:11)

Key word: Safety

Chapter 11. The *Lazarus* chapter.

> *I AM the resurrection and the life; he who*
> *believes in Me will live even if he dies,*
> *and everyone who lives and believes in*
> *Me will never die. Do you believe this?*
> (John 11:25-26)

Key word: Resurrection

Chapter 12. Here Christ closes up His ministry to the Jewish nation.

> *And I, if I am lifted up from the earth, will*
> *draw all men to Myself.* (John 12:32)

Key words: Salvation for all

Chapter 13. The *humility* chapter. Christ washes the feet of His disciples.

> *A new commandment I give to you, that you love one another, even as I have loved you, that you also love one another. By this all men will know that you are My disciples, if you have love for one another.* (John 13:34-35)

Key word: Teaching

Chapter 14. The *mansion* chapter.

> *I AM the way, and the truth, and the life; no one comes to the Father but through Me.* (John 14:6)

Key words: Peace and comfort

Chapter 15. The *fruit* chapter. The vine can only bear fruit through the branches.

> *I AM the vine, you are the branches; he who abides in Me and I in him, he bears much fruit, for apart from Me you can do nothing.* (John 15:5)

Key word: Joy

Chapter 16. The promise of the Holy Spirit. Here you find the secret of power and the Spirit of comfort and truth.

> *These things I have spoken to you, so that in Me you may have peace. In the world you*

*have tribulation, but take courage; I have
overcome the world.* (John 16:33)

Key word: Power

Chapter 17. This chapter contains the prayer of our Lord.

*I do not ask You to take them out of the
world, but to keep them from the evil one.*
(John 17:15)

Key word: Separation

Chapter 18. Christ is arrested. Despite the arrest and
trial of Jesus, He remained in full control, willingly and
humbly submitting in order to do His Father's will and
bring salvation to the lost world.

*So when He said to them, I AM He, they
drew back and fell to the ground.* (John 18:6)

Key words: In control

Chapter 19. Christ is crucified. Jesus died to pay for
our sins. We ought to live for Him. If this were the last
chapter in John, this would be a sad ending indeed; but
there is more to come!

*Therefore when Jesus had received the sour
wine, He said, It is finished! And He bowed
His head and gave up His spirit.* (John 19:30)

Key word: Death

Chapter 20. Christ rises from the dead.

Therefore many other signs Jesus also

*performed in the presence of the disciples,
which are not written in this book; but these
have been written so that you may believe
that Jesus is the Christ, the Son of God;
and that believing you may have life in His
name.* (John 20:30-31)

Key word: Resurrection

Chapter 21. Christ spends some time with His disciples again and invites them to dine with Him.

*This is the disciple who is testifying to these
things and wrote these things, and we know
that his testimony is true. And there are
also many other things which Jesus did,
which if they were written in detail, I suppose that even the world itself would not
contain the books that would be written.*
(John 21:24-25)

Key word: Ascension

Chapter 13

Types, Characters, and Names

Another way of studying the Bible is to take five great divisions: History, Type, Prophecy, Miracle, and Parable.

It is a very interesting thing to study the types of the Bible. A *type* is a representation of one thing that represents something else. For example, a sacrificial lamb might be a type, or representation, of Jesus. There are many types in the Old Testament that represent Jesus. Get a good book on the subject and you will be surprised to find out how interested you will become. The Bible is full of patterns and types of ourselves. A popular objection against the Bible is that it tells about the failings of men. We should, however, remember that the object of the Bible is not to tell how good men are, but how bad men can become good. More especially, the Bible is full of types of Christ. Types are foreshadowings, and wherever there is a shadow, there must be substance. As John McNeill says, "If I see the shadow of a dog, I know there's a dog around."

God seems to have chosen this means to teach the Israelites about the promised Messiah. All the laws, ceremonies, and institutions regarding Moses and the law and the tabernacle point to Christ and His death, burial, and resurrection. Read the book of Exodus and look for types of the Messiah. The enlightened eyes see Christ in all. For instance, the tabernacle was a type of the incarnation of Jesus. *And the Word became flesh, and dwelt among us* (John 1:14). The laver typified sanctification or purity. *That He might sanctify her, having cleansed her* [the church] *by the washing of water with the word* (Ephesians 5:26). The candlesticks typified Christ as the Light of the World. The showbread typified Christ as the Bread of Life. The high priest was always a type of Christ. Christ was called of God, as was Aaron. *He always lives to make intercession* (Hebrews 7:25). He was consecrated with an oath, and so on.

The Passover, the Day of Atonement, the smitten rock, the sacrifices, the city of refuge, and the brazen serpent all point to Christ's atoning work. Adam was a beautiful type. Think of the two Adams. One introduced sin and ruin into the world, and the other abolished it. So Cain stands as the representative natural man, and Abel as the spiritual man. Abel as a shepherd is a type of Christ, the heavenly Shepherd. There is no more beautiful type of Christ in the Bible than Joseph. He was hated by his brethren, he was stripped of his coat, he was sold, he was imprisoned, he gained favor, he had a gold chain about his neck, and every knee bowed before him. A comparison of the lives of Joseph and Jesus shows a startling similarity in their experience.

The disease of leprosy is a type of sin. It is incurable by man. It results in misery and affliction. It is treacherous in its nature, and from a small beginning it works complete ruin. It separates its victims from their fellow men, just as sin separates a man from God. *But your iniquities have made a separation between you and your God, and your sins have hidden His face from you so that He does not hear* (Isaiah 59:2). As Christ had power to cleanse the leper, so by the grace of God His blood cleanses us from all iniquity.

> *If we say that we have fellowship with Him and yet walk in the darkness, we lie and do not practice the truth; but if we walk in the Light as He Himself is in the Light, we have fellowship with one another, and the blood of Jesus His Son cleanses us from all sin.*
> (1 John 1:6-7)

- Adam represents man's innate sinfulness.

- Abel represents atonement.

- Enoch represents communion.

- Noah represents regeneration.

- Abraham represents faith.

- Isaac represents sonship.

- Jacob represents discipline and service.

- Joseph represents glory through suffering.

You see how studying the types in the Bible can be beneficial. Another good way to study the Bible is to study Bible characters; take them right from the cradle to the grave. You find that skeptics often take one particular part of a man's life – say, of the life of Jacob or of David – and judge their entire lives by that one part. Some say these men were not typical saints and that God did not punish them. If you go right through these men's lives, you will find that God did punish them according to the sins they committed.

A lady once said to me that she had trouble in reading the Bible, that she seemed not to feel the interest she ought. If you don't keep up your interest in one way, try another. Just keep reading it.

Another interesting study is the meaning of proper names. Every name in the Bible, especially Hebrew names, has a meaning of its own. Notice the difference between Abram ("a high father") and Abraham ("father of a multitude"), and you have a key to his life. Another example is Jacob ("supplanter") and Israel ("prince of God"). The names of Job's three daughters were Jemima ("a dove"), Kezia ("cassia"), and Kerenhappuch ("horn of paint"). These names signify beauty, so that Job's sore boils left no taint.

Chapter 14

Take God at His Word

I find some people now and then who boast that they have read the Bible through in so many months. Others read the Bible chapter by chapter and get through it in a year; that is good, but I think that sometimes it would be good to spend a year in just one book of the Bible. If I were going into a court of justice and wanted to win over the jury, I would want to get every witness I could to testify to the one point on which I wanted to convince the jury. I would not get them to testify to everything, but just to that one thing. So it should be with the Scriptures.

Sometimes it is good to study just one topic from the Bible. I once studied the word *love*, and I spent many weeks studying the passages in which it occurs, until at last I could not help loving people. I had been feeding so long on love that I was anxious to do good to everyone I met.

Take the word *sanctification*. I would rather take

my concordance and gather passages on sanctification and sit down for four or five days and study them thoroughly than have people tell me what they think about it.

I suppose that if all the time that I have prayed for faith was put together, it would be months. When I was president of the Young Men's Christian Association in Chicago, I used to say, "What we need is faith; if we only have faith, we can turn Chicago upside down," or rather, right side up. I thought that someday faith was going to come down and strike me like lightning; but faith did not seem to come. One day I read in Romans 10:17, *So faith comes from hearing, and hearing by the word of Christ.* Before, I had closed my Bible and prayed for faith; now I opened my Bible and began to study, and faith has been growing ever since.

Take justification – the doctrine that made Martin Luther such a power. *The righteous man shall live by faith* (Romans 1:17). When that thought flashed through Martin Luther's mind as he was in Rome ascending the twenty-eight Scala Sancta steps on his knees (although some people deny that this occurred), he rose and went forth to be a power among the nations of the earth. Justification places a man before God as if he had never sinned; he stands before God like Jesus Christ. Thank God, in Jesus Christ we can be perfect, but there is no perfection apart from Him. God looks in His account book and says, "Moody, your debts have all been paid by Another; there is nothing against you." People need to quit trusting in themselves and their religion and start trusting in Jesus.

In New England, there is perhaps no doctrine attacked so much as the atonement. The atonement is foreshadowed in the garden of Eden. There we see the innocent suffering for the guilty, the animals slain because of Adam's sin. We find it in Abraham's day, in Moses' day, and all through the books of Moses and the prophets. It is in the fifty-third chapter of Isaiah and in the prophecy of Daniel. Then we come to the Gospels, and Christ says, *For this reason the Father loves Me, because I lay down My life so that I may take it again. No one has taken it away from Me, but I lay it down on My own initiative. I have authority to lay it down, and I have authority to take it up again* (John 10:17-18).

The apostle Peter wrote: *For Christ also died for sins once for all, the just for the unjust, so that He might bring us to God, having been put to death in the flesh, but made alive in the spirit* (1 Peter 3:18).

People talk about conversion. What is conversion? The best way to find out is from the Bible. A good many don't believe in sudden conversions. You can die in a moment. Can't you receive eternal life in a moment?

When Mr. Ira Sankey and I were in Europe, a man preached a sermon against what he believed were the destructive doctrines that we were going to preach, one of which was sudden conversion. He said that conversion was a matter of time and growth. Do you know what I do when any man preaches against the doctrines I preach? I go to the Bible and find out what it says, and if I am right, I give them more of the same kind. I preached more on sudden conversion in that town than in any town I was in, in my life. How long did it take the Lord to convert that woman whom He met at the well of Sychar? How long did it take to convert that adulterous woman in the temple who was caught in the very act of adultery? How long to convert that woman who anointed His feet and wiped them with the hairs of her head? Didn't she leave with the word of God ringing in her ears, *Your faith has saved you; go in peace*? (Luke 7:50).

I would like to know how long it took the Lord to convert Zacchaeus. There was no sign of Zacchaeus being converted when he went up that sycamore tree, but he was converted by the time he came down, so he must have been converted between the branch and the ground. Pretty sudden work, wasn't it? But you say, "That is because Christ was there." Friends, they were converted a good deal faster after He went away than when He was here. Peter preached, and three thousand were converted in one day. Another time, after three o'clock in the afternoon, Peter and John healed a man at the gate of the temple and then went in and preached, and five thousand Jews were added to the church before night. That was rather sudden work.

Professor Drummond tells an illustration of a man going into one of our after-meetings and saying he wanted to become a Christian. "Well, my friend, what is the trouble?" He didn't want to tell him. He became greatly agitated. Finally, he said, "The fact is, I have overdrawn my account" – a polite way of saying he had been stealing.

"Did you take your employer's money?"

"Yes."

"How much?"

"I don't know. I never kept account of it."

"Well, do you think you stole fifteen hundred dollars last year?"

"I am afraid it is that much."

"Now, look here, sir, I don't believe in sudden conversions; don't steal more than a thousand dollars next year, and the year after that not more than five hundred, and in the course of the next few years you will get so that you won't steal any. If your employer catches you, tell him you are being converted, and you will get so that you won't steal any eventually."

My friends, that way of thinking is a waste of time. *He who steals must steal no longer*, the Bible says (Ephesians 4:28). It is an about-face.

Take another illustration. Here comes a man and he admits that he gets drunk every week. That man comes to a meeting and he wants to be converted. I say, "Don't you be in a hurry. I believe in doing the work gradually. Don't get drunk and knock your wife down more than once a month. Wouldn't it be refreshing to your wife to go a whole month without being knocked down? Once a month, only twelve times in a year! Wouldn't she be glad to have you converted in this new way? Only get drunk after a few years on the anniversary of your wedding, and at Christmas, and then it will be effective because it is gradual."

I detest all that kind of teaching. Let us go to the Bible and see what that old Book teaches. Let us believe it, and go and act as if we believed it too. Salvation is instantaneous. I admit that a man may be converted so that he cannot tell when he crossed the line between death and life, but I also believe a man may be a thief one moment and a saint the next. I believe a man may be as vile as hell itself one moment and be saved the next. Our churches are full of people who have never been converted, whose lives have never changed. There are many who have made decisions who have never been converted.

Christian growth is gradual, just as physical growth is; but a man passes from death unto everlasting life as quickly as an act of the mind: *He who believes in the Son has eternal life* (John 3:36).

People say they want to become heavenly minded. Well, read about heaven and talk about it. I once preached on heaven, and after the meeting a lady came to me and said, "Why, Mr. Moody, I didn't know there were so many verses in the Bible about heaven." And I hadn't mentioned even one out of a hundred. She was amazed that there was so much in the Bible about heaven.

When you are away from home, you look for news about home! You skip everything in the daily paper until your eye catches the name of your own town or country. The Christian's home is in heaven. The Scriptures contain our title deeds to everything we will be worth when we die. If a will has your name in it, it is no longer a meaningless document to you. Why, then, do not Christians take more interest in the Bible?

Then again, people say they don't believe in revivals. There's not a denomination in the world that didn't spring from a revival. The Catholic and Episcopal churches claim to be the apostolic churches and to have sprung from Pentecost, the Lutheran church from Martin Luther, and so on. They all sprang out of revivals, and yet people talk against revivals! I'd as soon talk against my mother as against a revival. Wasn't the country revived under John the Baptist? Wasn't it under Christ's teachings? People think that because a number of superficial cases of conversion occur at revivals, that therefore revivals ought to be avoided. They forget the parable of the sower (Matthew 13), where Jesus Himself warns us of emotional hearers who receive the word with joy, but soon fall away. If only one out of every four hearers is truly converted, as in the parable, the revival has done much good.

Suppose you spend a month studying regeneration, or the kingdom of God, or the church in the New Testament, or the divinity of Christ, or the Lord's Day, or holiness, or the attributes of God. It will help you in your own spiritual life, and you will become a workman who need not be ashamed, rightly dividing the Word of Truth.

Make a study of the Holy Spirit. There are probably five hundred passages on the Holy Spirit, and what you ought to do is study this subject for yourself. Take the return of our Lord. I know it is a debated subject. Some say He is to come at the end of the millennium, while others say He will come back before the millennium. What we want is to know what the Bible says. Why not go to the Bible and study it for yourself? It will be worth more to you than anything you get from anyone else. Put down the fiction books and get to the Word of Truth.

Study what the Bible says about separation – being separate from the world. I believe that a Christian should lead a separated life. The line between the church and the world is almost obliterated today. I have no sympathy with the idea that you must hunt up a church record in order to find out whether a man is a member of the church or not. A man ought to live so that everybody will know he is a Christian. The Bible tells us to lead a separated life. You may lose influence, but you will gain it at the same time.

I suppose Daniel was the most unpopular man in Babylon at a certain time, but thank God, he has outlived all the other men of his time. Who were the chief men of Babylon? We do not remember the others, but we remember Daniel. When God wanted any work done in Babylon, He knew where to find someone to do it. You can be in the world, but not of it. Christ didn't take His disciples out of the world, but He prayed that they might be kept from evil (John 17). A ship in the water is all right, but when the water gets into the ship, then look out. A worldly Christian is just like a wrecked vessel at sea.

I remember once when I spent some time studying the grace of God. I didn't know the difference between law and grace. When that truth dawned upon me and I saw the difference, I studied for a whole week on grace and I got so filled that I couldn't stay in the house. I said to the first man I met, "Do you know anything about the grace of God?" He thought I was a lunatic, but I just poured out for about an hour on the grace of God.

Study the subject of prayer. In his sermon "The Two Guards, Praying and Watching," Charles Spurgeon said:

> For real business at the mercy seat, give me a homemade prayer, a prayer that comes out of the depths of my heart, not because I invented it, but because God the Holy Spirit put it there, and gave it such a living force that I could not help letting it come out. Though your words are broken, and your sentences are disconnected, if your desires are earnest, if they are like coals of juniper, burning with a vehement flame, God will not mind how they find expression. If you have no words, perhaps you will pray better without them. There are prayers that break the backs of words; they are too heavy for any human language to carry.

Some people say, "I do not believe in assurance." I never knew anybody who read the Bible who did not believe in assurance. This Book teaches nothing else. Paul says, *I know whom I have believed* (2 Timothy 1:12). Job says, *I know that my Redeemer lives* (Job 19:25). It is not "I hope" or "I trust," but "I know."

The best book on assurance was written by a man named John, and it is found in the back part of the Bible. John wrote an epistle on this subject. We call it 1 John. Now if you turn to John 20:31, you will find that it says, *These have been written so that you may believe that Jesus is the Christ, the Son of God; and that believing you may have life in His name.* Then if you turn to 1 John 5:13, you will read this: *These things I have written to you who believe in the name of the Son of God, so that you may know that you have eternal life.* That whole epistle is written on assurance. I have no doubt John had found some people who questioned assurance and doubted whether they were saved, and so he took up his pen and said, "I will settle that question," and he wrote that last verse in the twentieth chapter of his gospel.

I have heard some people say that they were not able to know if they were saved. They had heard the minister say that no one could know whether they were saved or not, and they believed what the minister said instead of what the Word of God said. Others read the Bible to make it fit in and prove their favorite creed or notions, and if it does not do so, they will not read it anymore. It has been well said that we must not read the Bible by the blue light of Presbyterianism, nor by the red light of Methodism, nor by the violet light of Episcopalianism, but by the light of the Spirit of God. If you will take up your Bible and study *assurance* for a week, you will soon see it is your privilege to know that you are a child of God.

Then take the promises of God. Let a man feed for a month on the promises of God, and he will not talk about his poverty and how downcast he is and what trouble he has day by day. You hear people say, "Oh, how inadequate I am! I am not able to know God better." My friends, it is not their inadequacy, but it is their laziness. If you would only go from Genesis to Revelation and see all the promises made by God to Abraham, to

Isaac, to Jacob, to the Jews and the Gentiles, and to all His people everywhere; if you would spend a month feeding on the precious promises of God, you would not go about with your heads hanging down like bulrushes, complaining about how poor you are, but you would lift up your heads with confidence and proclaim the riches of His grace, because you could not help it.

After the Chicago fire, a man came up to me and said in a sympathizing tone, "Moody, I understand you lost everything in the Chicago fire."

"Well then," I said, "someone has misinformed you."

"Indeed! Why, I was told you had lost all."

"No, it is a mistake," I said, "quite a mistake."

"Have you got much left, then?" asked my friend.

"Yes," I replied, "I have got much more left than I lost, though I cannot tell how much I have lost."

"Well, I am glad of it, Moody; I did not know you were that rich before the fire."

"Yes," said I, "I am a good deal richer than you could conceive; and here is my title deed: *He who overcomes will inherit these things*" (Revelation 21:7).

They say the Rothschilds cannot tell how much they are worth, and that is just my case. All things in the world are mine; I am a joint heir with Jesus, the Son of God. Someone has said, "God makes a promise, faith believes it, hope anticipates it, and patience quietly awaits it."

Chapter 15

One Word at a Time

Another way to study the Bible is to take one word and follow it up with the help of a concordance, or take just one word that runs through a book. Some time ago, I was wonderfully blessed by taking the seven *Blessed*s of the book of Revelation. If God did not wish us to understand the book of Revelation, He would not have given it to us at all. A good many people say it is so dark and mysterious that common readers cannot understand it. Let us only keep digging away at it, and we will start to understand it better. Someone says it is the only book in the Bible that tells about the Devil being chained, and since the Devil knows that, he goes up and down Christendom and says, "It is no use reading Revelation; you cannot understand the book. It is too hard for you." The fact is, he does not want you to understand about his own defeat. Just look at the *Blessed*s the book contains:

1. *Blessed is he who reads and those who hear the words of the prophecy, and heed the things which are written in it; for the time is near.* (Revelation 1:3)

2. *Blessed are the dead who die in the Lord from now on! Yes, says the Spirit, so that they may rest from their labors, for their deeds follow with them.* (Revelation 14:13)

3. *Blessed is the one who stays awake and keeps his clothes.* (Revelation 16:15)

4. *Blessed are those who are invited to the marriage supper of the Lamb.* (Revelation 19:9)

5. *Blessed and holy is the one who has a part in the first resurrection; over these the second death has no power, but they will be priests of God and of Christ and will reign with Him for a thousand years.* (Revelation 20:6)

6. *Blessed is he who heeds the words of the prophecy of this book.* (Revelation 22:7)

7. *Blessed are those who wash their robes, so that they may have the right to the tree of life, and may enter by the gates into the city.* (Revelation 22:14)

Or you may take the eight *overcomes* in Revelation, and you will be wonderfully blessed by them. They take you right up to the throne of heaven; by them you climb to the throne of God.

I have been greatly blessed by going through the *believing*s of John. Every chapter but three speaks of believing. As I said before, John wrote his gospel that we might believe. All through it is "Believe! Believe!" If you want to persuade a man that Christ is the Son of God, John's gospel is the book for him.

Take the eight *precious* things in Peter's epistles, the seven *walk*s of the epistle to the Ephesians, or the five *much more*s of Romans 5. Study the three *received*s of John 1 and the eight *heart*s in Proverbs 23.

Examine *the fear of the Lord* in Proverbs:

The fear of the LORD is to hate evil. (8:13)

The fear of the LORD is the beginning of wisdom. (9:10)

The fear of the LORD prolongs life. (10:27)

In the fear of the LORD there is strong confidence. (14:26)

The fear of the LORD is a fountain of life. (14:27)

Better is a little with the fear of the LORD than great treasure and turmoil with it. (15:16)

The fear of the LORD is the instruction for wisdom. (15:33)

By the fear of the LORD one keeps away from evil. (16:6)

*The fear of the LORD leads to life, so that
one may sleep satisfied.* (19:23)

*The reward of humility and the fear of the
LORD are riches, honor and life.* (22:4)

Live in the fear of the LORD always. (23:17)

A friend gave me some key words recently. He said Peter
wrote about hope: *When the Chief Shepherd appears*
(1 Peter 5:4). The keynote of Paul's writings seemed to
be faith, and that of John's, love. Faith, hope, and love
were the characteristics of the three men, the keynotes
to the whole of their teachings. James wrote of good
works, and Jude of apostasy.

For the general epistles of Paul, someone suggested
that Paul emphasizes the phrase *in Christ*. In the book
of Romans, we find justification by faith *in Christ*.
Corinthians presents sanctification *in Christ*. In the
book of Galatians, we see adoption or liberty *in Christ*.
Ephesians presents fullness *in Christ*; Philippians, consolation *in Christ*. In Colossians, we have completeness
in Christ. Thessalonians gives us hope *in Christ*.

Chapter 16

Mark My Word

D on't be afraid to borrow and lend Bibles. Some
time ago, a man wanted to take my Bible home
to get a few things out of it, and when he returned it,
I found this noted in it:

*Justification: a change of state, a new standing
before God.*

*Repentance: a change of mind, a new mind
about God.*

*Regeneration: a change of nature, a new heart
from God.*

Conversion: a change of life, a new life for God.

*Adoption: a change of family, a new relationship
towards God.*

*Sanctification: a change of service, separation
unto God.*

Glorification: a new state, a new condition with God.

In the same handwriting I found these lines:

Jesus only:

The light of heaven is the face of Jesus.

The joy of heaven is the presence of Jesus.

The melody of heaven is the name of Jesus.

The theme of heaven is the work of Jesus.

The employment of heaven is the service of Jesus.

The fullness of heaven is Jesus Himself.

The duration of heaven is the eternity of Jesus.

Sir Francis Bacon said that some books are to be tasted, some to be swallowed, and some to be chewed and digested. The Bible is one that you can never exhaust. It is like a bottomless well. You can always find fresh truths gushing forth from its pages. That is the great fascination of constant and earnest Bible study. This is also the reason for marking your Bible. Unless you have an uncommon memory, you cannot remember for long the good things you hear. If you trust your ears alone, those good things you hear will escape you in a day or two; but if you mark your Bible and enlist the aid of your eyes, you will never lose them. The same applies to what you read.

Bible marking should be made the servant of the memory. If properly done, it sharpens the memory rather than dulls it, because it gives prominence to certain things that catch the eye, which by constant reading you get to learn of by heart. It helps you to locate texts. It saves you the trouble of writing out notes for your lessons or discussions. Once in the margin, it is always ready.

I have carried one Bible with me a great many years. It is worth a good deal to me, because I have so many passages marked in it, that if I am called upon to speak at any time, I am ready. I have little words marked in the margins, and they are a sermon to me. Whether I speak about faith, hope, charity, assurance, or any subject whatsoever, it all comes back to me; and however unexpectedly I am called upon to preach, I am always ready.

Every child of God ought to be like a soldier and always hold himself in readiness. If the Queen of England's army was ordered to India tomorrow, her soldiers would be ready for the journey; but soldiers in God's army cannot be ready if they do not study the Bible. Whenever you hear a good thing, just write it down, because if it is good for you, it will be good for somebody else, and we should pass the coin of heaven around just as we do with money in this life. A single dollar can travel all over this land, and the good we get out of God's Word can do the same. Don't keep it to yourself.

People tell me they have nothing to say. *For the mouth speaks out of that which fills the heart* (Matthew 12:34). Get full of Scripture, and then you can't help but say it. It says itself. Keep the world out of your heart by getting full of something else. Some people have no problem talking about sports, but they cannot talk much about the Scriptures. That tells you what is in their hearts. A man once tried to build a flying machine. He made some wings and filled them with gas. He said he couldn't quite fly, but the gas was lighter than the air and it helped him over lots of obstructions. When you get these heavenly truths, they are lighter than the air down here and they help you over trouble.

Bible marking makes the Bible a new book to you. If there was a white birch tree within a quarter of a mile of your childhood home, you would remember it all your life. Mark your Bible, and instead of it being dry and uninteresting, it will become a beautiful book to you. What you see makes a more lasting impression on your memory than what you hear.

There are many methods of marking. Some people use six or eight colored inks or pencils. They use black to mark texts that refer to sin, red for all references to the cross, blue for all references to heaven, and so on. Others invent symbols. When there is any reference to the cross, they put a little cross in the margin. Some write G, meaning the gospel.

There is the danger of overdoing this and making your marks more prominent than the Bible itself. If the system is complicated, it becomes a burden and you are likely to get confused; it is then easier to remember the text than the meaning of your marks.

Black ink is good enough for most purposes. I use no other, except I sometimes use red ink to draw attention to "the blood."

The simplest way to mark is to underline the words or to make a stroke alongside the verse. Another good way is to go over the printed letters with your pen, making the letters thicker. The word will then stand out like heavier type. Mark the word *only* in Psalm 62 in this way.

> *My soul waits in silence for God **only**; From Him is my salvation. He **only** is my rock and my salvation, my stronghold; I shall not be greatly shaken. How long will you assail a man, that you may murder him, all of you, like a leaning wall, like a tottering fence? They have counseled **only** to thrust him down from his high position; They delight in falsehood; They bless with their mouth, But inwardly they curse. Selah. My soul, wait in silence for God **only**, for my hope is from Him. He **only** is my rock and my salvation, my stronghold; I shall not be shaken.* (Psalm 62:1-6)

When any word or phrase is often repeated in a chapter or book, put consecutive numbers in the margin beside the text. Thus, in the second chapter of Habakkuk, we find five *woe*s against five common sins: (1) verse 6, (2) verse 9, (3) verse 12, (4) verse 15, and (5) verse 19. Number the ten plagues in this way.

When there is a succession of promises or commands in a verse, it is better to write small numbers at the beginning of each separate promise. Thus, there is a sevenfold promise to Abraham in Genesis 12:2-3: (1) *I will make you a great nation*, (2) *and I will bless you* (3) *and make your name great*; (4) *and you shall be a blessing.* (5) *And I will bless those who bless you* (6)

and the one who curses you I will curse, (7) a*nd in you
all the families of the earth will be blessed.*
In Proverbs 1:22, we have (1) simple ones, (2) scorners,
and (3) fools.

I also find it helpful to mark the following:

1. Cross-references. Next to Genesis 1:1, write: "Through
faith, Hebrews 11:3," because there we read: *By faith we
understand that the worlds were prepared by the word of
God.* Next to Genesis 28:12 write: "An answer to prayer,
Genesis 35:3." Next to Matthew 6:33 write: "1 Kings 3:13
and Luke 10:42," which give illustrations of seeking
the kingdom of God first. Beside Genesis 37:7 write:
"Genesis 50:18," which is the fulfillment of the dream.

2. Railroad connections. These are connections made
by fine lines running across the page. In Daniel 6, connect *may he deliver* (v. 16), *able to deliver* (v. 20), and
delivered (v. 27). In Psalm 66, connect *come and see*
(v. 5) with *come and hear* (v. 16).

3. Words that have changed their meaning, or where
you can explain a difficulty, or where the English does
not bring out the full meaning of the original, as happens sometimes with the names of God.

4. Unfortunate divisions of chapters. The last verse of
John 7 reads: *Everyone went to his home.* Chapter 8
begins: *Jesus went to the Mount of Olives.* The chapter
should not be divided here.

5. Make a note of any text that marks a religious crisis in your life. I once heard the Rev. F. B. Meyer preach on 1 Corinthians 1:9, and he asked his hearers to write in their Bibles that they were that day *called into the fellowship with his Son, Jesus Christ our Lord.*

When a preacher gives out a text and preaches a sermon that affects you, mark the text in your Bible; put a few words in the margin, such as keywords that will bring back the whole sermon again. By that plan of making a few marginal notes, I can remember sermons I heard years and years ago. Every man ought to take down some of the preacher's words and ideas, and then go and preach them again to others. We ought to have four ears: two for ourselves and two for other people. Then, if you are in a new town and have nothing else to say, jump up and say, "I heard someone say such and such." People should always be glad to hear you if you give them heavenly food. The world is perishing for lack of it.

Some years ago, I heard an Englishman in Chicago preach from a curious text: *Four things are small on the earth, but they are exceedingly wise* (Proverbs 30:24). "Well," I said to myself, "what will you make of these little things? I have seen them many times."

Then he went on speaking: *The ants are not a strong people, but they prepare their food in the summer.* He said God's people are like the ants.

"Well," I thought, "I have seen many of them, but I never saw one like me."

"They are like the ants," he said, "because they are laying up treasure in heaven, and preparing for the future; but the world rushes madly on and forgets all about God's command to lay up for ourselves incorruptible treasures."

The shephanim are not mighty people, yet they make their houses in the rocks. He said, "The shephanim are very weak things; if you were to throw a stick at one of them, you could kill it; but they are very wise, for they build their houses in rocks, where they are out of harm's way. God's people are very wise, although very feeble; for they build on the Rock of Ages, and that Rock is Christ."

"Well," I said, "I am certainly like the shephanim."

Then came the next verse: *The locusts have no king, yet all of them go out in ranks.* I wondered what he was going to make of that.

"God's people," he said, "have no king down here. The world said, 'Caesar is our king,' but he is not *our* king; our king is the Lord of Hosts. The locusts went out in ranks, or groups; so do God's people. Here is a Presbyterian group, here an Episcopalian group, here a Methodist group, and so on; but in His time, the great King will come and catch up all these separate groups, and they will all be one: one fold and one Shepherd."

And when I heard that explanation, I said; "I would like to be like the locusts." I have become so sick, my friends, of this miserable sectarianism, that I wish it could all be swept away. We have enough denominations and division.

The preacher continued: *The spider taketh hold with her hands, and is in kings' palaces* (KJV).

When he got to the spider, I said, "I don't like that at all; I don't like the idea of being compared to a spider."

"But," he said, "if you go into a king's palace, there is the spider hanging on his delicate web, looking down with scorn and contempt on the gold-filled elaborate room; he is laying hold of things above. And so every child of God ought to be like the spider and lay hold of the unseen things of God. You see then, my brethren, we who are God's people are like the ants, the conies, the locusts, and the spiders: little things, but exceedingly wise." I put that down in the margin of my Bible, and the recollection of it does me as much good now as when I first heard it.

A friend of mine was in Edinburgh, and he heard one of the leading Scotch Presbyterian ministers. He had been preaching from Revelation 1:7: *Every eye shall see him*, and he closed by saying, "Yes, every eye. Adam will see Him, and when he does, he will say, 'This is He who was promised to me in that dark day when I fell'; Abraham will see Him and will say, 'This is He whom I saw afar off, but now face to face'; Mary will see Him, and she will sing her song with new interest. And I too will see Him, and when I do, I will sing, 'Rock of Ages, cleft for me, let me hide myself in Thee.'"

Here are some more examples that might be helpful to you.

Turn to Exodus 6:6-8. In these verses, we find seven *I will*s.

> *Say, therefore, to the sons of Israel, I am the LORD, and I **will** bring you out from under*

*the burdens of the Egyptians, and I **will**
deliver you from their bondage. I **will** also
redeem you with an outstretched arm and
with great judgments. Then I **will** take you
for My people, and I **will** be your God; and
you shall know that I am the LORD your
God, who brought you out from under the
burdens of the Egyptians. I **will** bring you to
the land which I swore to give to Abraham,
Isaac, and Jacob, and I **will** give it to you for
a possession; I am the LORD.*

Look now at Isaiah 41:10. *Do not fear, for I am with you;
Do not anxiously look about you, for I am your God. I
will strengthen you, surely I will help you, surely I will
uphold you with My righteous right hand.*

Notice what God says:

- He is with His servant.

- He is his God.

- He will strengthen.

- He will help.

- He will uphold.

Turn to Psalm 103:2: *Bless the LORD, O my soul, and
forget none of His benefits.* If you cannot remember all
of these benefits, remember what you can. In the next
three verses, there are five things to be sure to notice
and remember:

*Who pardons all your iniquities, Who heals
all your diseases; Who redeems your life from*

*the pit, Who crowns you with lovingkind-
ness and compassion; Who satisfies your
years with good things, so that your youth is
renewed like the eagle.* (Psalm 103:3-5)

- God *pardons* all your iniquities.

- God *heals* all your diseases.

- God *redeems* your life from destruction.

- God *crowns* you with mercy and
  compassion.

- God *satisfies* your mouth with good
  things.

Let's look at Psalm 23. I suppose I have heard as many
good sermons on the twenty-third psalm as on any other
six verses in the Bible. I wish I had begun to take notes
upon them years ago when I heard the first one. Things
slip away from you when you get to be fifty years of
age. Young people had better go into training at once.

*The LORD is my shepherd, I shall not want.
He makes me lie down in green pastures;
He leads me beside quiet waters. He restores
my soul; He guides me in the paths of righteousness for His name's sake. Even though
I walk through the valley of the shadow of
death, I fear no evil, for You are with me;
Your rod and Your staff, they comfort me
You prepare a table before me in the presence of my enemies; You have anointed my
head with oil; My cup overflows. Surely*

goodness and lovingkindness will follow me
all the days of my life, and I will dwell in the
house of the LORD forever. (Psalm 23)

What we can write down about this psalm:

- With me: the LORD

- Beneath me: green pastures

- Beside me: still waters

- Before me: a table

- Around me: my enemies

- After me: goodness and mercy

- Ahead of me: the house of the Lord

"Blessed is the day," says an old preacher, "when Psalm twenty-three was born!" It has been more used than almost any other passage in the Bible.

Here is another way to look at Psalm 23:

Verse 1: A happy life

Verse 4: A happy death

Verse 6: A happy eternity

Take Psalm 102:6-7: *I resemble a pelican of*
the wilderness; I have become like an owl of
the waste places. I lie awake, I have become
like a lonely bird on a housetop.

This seems strange until you reflect that a pelican carries its food with it, the owl keeps its eyes open at night, and the sparrow watches alone. So, the Christian must carry his food, the Bible, with him, and he must keep his eyes open and watch alone.

Turn to Isaiah 32 and mark four things that God promises in verse 2: *Each will be like a refuge from the wind and a shelter from the storm, like streams of water in a dry country, like the shade of a huge rock in a parched land.*

Here we have:

- The hiding place from danger
- The cover from the tempest
- The rivers of water
- The Rock of Ages

In the third and fourth verses of the same chapter we read: *Then the eyes of those who see will not be blinded, and the ears of those who hear will listen. The mind of the hasty will discern the truth, and the tongue of the stammerers will hasten to speak clearly.*

We have eyes, ears, heart, and tongue, all ready to pay homage to the King of Righteousness.

Now turn to John 4:47-53 in the New Testament:

> *When he heard that Jesus had come out of Judea into Galilee, he went to Him and was imploring Him to come down and heal his son; for he was at the point of death. So Jesus said to him, Unless you people see signs and wonders, you simply will not believe. The royal official said to Him, Sir, come down before my child dies. Jesus said to him, Go; your son lives. The man believed the word*

*that Jesus spoke to him and started off. As
he was now going down, his slaves met him,
saying that his son was living. So he inquired
of them the hour when he began to get better. Then they said to him, Yesterday at the
seventh hour the fever left him. So the father
knew that it was at that hour in which Jesus
said to him, Your son lives; and he himself
believed and his whole household.*

- The nobleman *heard* about Jesus.

- The nobleman *went* unto Him.

- The nobleman *implored* Him.

- The nobleman *believed* Him.

- The nobleman *knew* that his prayer was answered.

Look at Matthew 11:28-30:

*Come to Me, all who are weary and heavy-
laden, and I will give you rest. Take My
yoke upon you and learn from Me, for I am
gentle and humble in heart, and you will
find rest for your souls. For My yoke is easy
and My burden is light.*

Someone has said these verses contain the only description we have of Christ's heart.

- Something to do: come to Jesus

- Something to leave: your burden

- Something to take: His yoke

- Something to find: rest for your soul

Let's look at one more – John 14:6: *I AM the way, and the truth, and the life.*

- The way: follow Me

- The truth: learn of Me

- The life: abide in Me

Here are some suggestions that might be beneficial to you:

- Do not buy a Bible that you are unwilling to mark and use. An interleaved Bible gives more room for notes.

- Be precise and concise; for example, Nehemiah 13:18: "A warning from history."

- Never mark anything because you saw it in someone else's Bible. If it does not come home to you, if you not understand it, do not mark it down.

- Never pass a nugget by without trying to grasp it. Then mark it down.

Chapter 17

Personal Work for God

Dealing with people personally is of vital importance. No one can tell how many people have
been lost to the kingdom of God through lack of following up the preaching of the gospel by personal work.
It is deplorable how few church members are qualified
to deal with those who are inquiring about salvation,
yet that is the very work in which they ought most
efficiently to aid the pastor.

People are not usually converted under the preaching of the minister. It is in the inquiry meeting (where
those seeking Christ meet after the preaching to discuss
their spiritual needs more personally), that they are
most likely to be brought to Christ. They are perhaps
awakened under the minister, but God generally uses
some one person to point out the way of salvation and
bring the concerned to Jesus. Some people can't see the
use of inquiry meetings. They think they are something
new and that we haven't any authority for them; but they

are no innovation. We read about them all through the Bible. When John the Baptist was preaching, he was interrupted. It would be a good thing if people would interrupt the minister now and then in the middle of some metaphysical sermon and ask what he means. The only way to make sure that people understand what he is talking about is to let them ask questions. I don't know what some men, who have their whole sermon written out, would do if someone got up and asked, "What must I do to be saved?" Yet such questions would do more good than anything else you could have. They would awaken a spirit of inquiry. Some of Christ's sweetest teachings were called forth by questions.

There ought to be three kinds of services in all churches: (1) One for worship, to offer praise, and to wait on the Lord in prayer; (2) One for teaching, and at these services there needn't be a word to the unconverted (although some men never close any meeting without presenting the gospel), but let the teaching be for the church people; and (3) One for preaching the gospel. Sunday morning is the best time for teaching, but Sunday night is the best night in the whole week, of the regular church services, to preach the simple gospel of the Son of God. When you have preached the simple gospel and have felt the power of the unseen world and there are souls trembling in the balance, don't say, as I have heard good ministers say, "*If* there are any in this place concerned about their souls, I will be in the pastor's study on Friday night and will be glad to see them." By that time, the chances are that the impression will be all wiped out. Deal with them that night, before the Devil snatches away the good seed. Wherever the gospel is proclaimed, there should be an expectation of immediate results; if this were the case, the church of Christ would be in a constant state of grace.

Now when the meeting of the synagogue had broken up, many of the Jews and of the God-fearing proselytes followed Paul and Barnabas, who, speaking to them, were urging them to continue in the grace of God (Acts 13:43). How much would Paul and Barnabas have accomplished if they had pronounced the benediction and sent these people home? It is something to weep over that we have thousands and thousands of church members who are good for nothing towards extending the kingdom of God. They understand sports, fairs, and current events, but when you ask them to sit down and show a man or woman the way into God's kingdom, they say, "Oh, I am not able to do that. Let the deacons do it, or someone else." They might even invite people to church to let the pastor talk to them about Jesus, but they cannot or will not take them to Jesus themselves. It is all wrong. The church ought to be educated on this very point. There are a great many church members who are just hobbling about on crutches. They can just make out that they are saved, and they imagine that is all that constitutes a Christian. As far as helping others is concerned, that never enters their heads. They think if they can get along themselves, they are doing amazingly well. They have no idea what the Holy Spirit wants to do through them.

No matter how weak you are, God can use you, and you do not know what a stream of salvation you may set in motion. John the Baptist was a young man when he died, but he led Andrew to Christ, and Andrew led Peter, and so the river flowed on.

In the closing pages of this book, I want to give some hints in regard to passing on the good to others, and so profiting them by your knowledge of the Bible. Every believer, whether minister or layman, is duty bound to spread the gospel. *Go into all the world and preach the gospel to all creation* was the wide command of our parting Savior to His disciples (Mark 16:15).

There are many Bible students, however, who utterly neglect the command. They are like sponges, always sucking in the Water of Life, but never imparting it to thirsty souls around them. When was the last time you spoke to someone about Jesus? A clergyman used to go hunting, and when his bishop reproved him, he said he never went hunting when he was on duty.

"When is a clergyman off duty?" asked the bishop.

And so with every Christian: when is he off duty?

To be ready with a promise for the dying, a word of hope for the bereaved and afflicted, of encouragement for the downhearted, or a word of advice for the anxious is a great accomplishment. The opportunities to be useful in these ways are numerous. Not only in inquiry meetings and church work, but the opening also constantly occurs in our everyday contact with others. A word, a look, a handshake, or a prayer may have an unending influence for good.

"Is your father at home?" asked a gentleman of a doctor's child.

"No," he said, "he's away."

"Where can I find him?"

"Well," he said, "you've got to look for him in some place where people are sick or hurt, or something like that. I don't know where he is, but he's helping somewhere."

That ought to be the spirit animating every follower of Him who went about doing good.

I admit that one cannot lay down specific rules in dealing with individuals about their religious condition. Tin soldiers are exactly alike, but people are not. Matthew was a lot different from Paul. The people we deal with may be widely different. What would be medicine for one might be poison for another. In the fifteenth chapter of Luke, the elder son and the younger son were exactly opposite. What would have been good counsel for one might have been ruin to the other. God never made two persons to look alike. If we had made people, we probably would have made them all alike, even if we had to crush some bones to get them into the mold. But that is not God's way. There is infinite variety in the universe. The Philippian jailer required specific treatment. Christ dealt with Nicodemus one way and with the woman at the well another way.

In dealing with inquirers, it is a great mistake to tell your conversion experience. Experience may have its place, but I don't think it has its place when we are dealing with inquirers. If you first tell an inquirer your own conversion experience, he will think that his experience must exactly match yours. He doesn't want your experience; he wants one of his own.

Suppose Bartimaeus had gone to Jerusalem to the man who was born blind, and said:

"Tell us how the Lord cured you."

The Jerusalem man might have said, "He just spit on the ground and anointed my eyes with the clay."

"No!" says Bartimaeus. "I don't believe you ever got your sight at all. Who ever heard of being healed that way? That is not how Jesus healed me. To fill a man's eyes with clay is enough to make you blind!"

Both men were blind, but they were not cured in the same way. A great many men are kept out of the kingdom of God because they are looking for somebody else's experience – the experience their grandmother had, their aunt, or someone else in the family.

It is also very important to deal with one person at a time. A doctor doesn't give cod liver oil for all complaints. "No," he says, "I must seek what each one needs." He looks at the tongue and inquires into the symptoms. One person may have the flu, another typhoid fever, and another may have a stomachache. We need to be able to read our Bibles and to read human nature too.

Those do best who do not run from one person to another in an inquiry meeting, offering words of encouragement everywhere. They would do better by going to only one or two persons. We are building for eternity, and that can take time. The work will not then be superficial. Try first to win the person's confidence, and then your words will have more weight. Use great tact in approaching the subject.

It will be very helpful to realize the different classes or conditions of people as much as possible, and bring certain passages of Scripture to bear upon these classes. Don't just repeat a verse that you have seen in a book, unless you personally understand and know the meaning and application of that verse. By all means, use suggestions from outside sources, but just as David could not fight in Saul's armor, the verse that someone else used in a specific situation might not be the right verse for you to use in your situation. Look how varied the counsel of Jesus was. He aimed His words specifically toward each individual with whom He dealt.

It is better to be familiar with a few passages than to have a hazy and incomplete idea of a large number of verses. Look at the classes below. What are some verses that would be good for each class of inquirer? What is helpful to one class might not be what is needed by another.

The following classifications may be found helpful:

1. Believers who lack assurance, who are in darkness because they have sinned, who neglect prayer, Bible study, and other means of grace, who are in darkness because of an unforgiving spirit, who are timid or ashamed to confess Christ openly, who are not engaged in active work for the Master, who lack strength to resist temptation and to stand fast in time of trial, and who are not growing in grace.

2. Believers who have backslidden.

3. Those who are deeply convicted of sin and are seeking salvation.

4. Those who have difficulties of various kinds. Many believe that they are so sinful that God will not accept them, that they have sinned away their opportunities and now it is too late, that the gospel was never intended for them. Others are kept back by honest doubts regarding the divinity of Christ or the genuineness of the Bible. Others again are troubled by the mysteries of the Bible, the doctrines of election, instant conversion, or some other difficulty, or they say they have sought Christ in vain, that they have tried and failed. A large class is in great trouble about feelings.

5. Those who make excuses. There is a wide difference between a person who has a *reason* and one who has an *excuse* to offer. The most common excuses are that there are many inconsistent Christians and hypocrites in the church, that it would cost too much to become a Christian, that they could not continue in their present way of life, that they expect to become Christians someday, or that their companions hold them back or would cast them off if they were converted.

6. Those who are not convicted of sin. Some are deliberately sinful; they want to "see life," to "sow their wild oats." Others are thoughtless. Others again are simply ignorant of Jesus Christ and His work.

7. A large number do not feel their need of a Savior because they are self-righteous, trusting in their own morality and good works.

8. Those who hold hostile creeds, embracing sectarians, spiritualists, infidels, atheists, agnostics, etc.

Always use your Bible in personal dealing. Do not trust your memory, but make the person read the verse for himself. Do not use printed slips or books. So, if convenient, always carry a Bible or New Testament with you.

It is a good thing to get someone to pray (if convenient), but don't get him there before he is ready. Remember, it is the Holy Spirit and not you who does the converting and who gives new life. You may have to talk with a person two hours before you can get him that far along. When you think he is about ready, say to him, "Let's ask God to help us understand this point." Sometimes a few minutes in prayer has done more for a man than two hours in talk. When the Spirit of God has led him so far that he is willing to have you pray with him, he is not very far from the kingdom. Ask him to pray for himself. If he does not want to pray, let him use a Bible prayer; get him to repeat it. For example, *Lord, help me* (Matthew 15:25). Tell the man, "If the Lord helped that poor woman, He will help you if you make the same prayer with the same heart. He will give you a new heart if you pray from the heart." Don't send a man home to pray. Of course, he should pray at home, but I would rather get his lips open at once. It is a good thing for a man to hear his own voice in prayer. It is a good thing for him to cry out, *God, be merciful to me, the sinner* (Luke 18:13).

Urge an immediate decision, but never tell a man he is converted. Never tell him he is saved. Let the

Holy Spirit reveal that to him. You can shoot a man and see that he is dead, but you cannot see when a man receives eternal life. You cannot afford to deceive anyone about this great question, but you can help his faith and trust, and lead him aright. There are many people who wrongly think that they are on the way to heaven simply because a well-meaning person or even a pastor has told them that they are now saved simply because they "made a decision" or said a prayer; but they have never repented and their hearts have never been made new by the Spirit of God.

Always be prepared to do personal work. When war was declared between France and Germany, Count von Moltke, the German general, was prepared for it. Word was brought to him late at night, after he had gone to bed. "Very well," he said to the messenger, "the third portfolio on the left" (where he had his battle plans); and he went to sleep again.

Do the work boldly. Don't deal with a person of the opposite gender, if it can be otherwise arranged. Make all efforts to answer for poor, struggling souls the question that is of all importance to them: *What must I do to be saved?* (Acts 16:30).

Chapter 18

Summary of Suggestions

1 Have for constant use a reference Bible, a concordance, and a topical Bible.

2. Always carry a Bible or New Testament in your pocket, and do not be ashamed of people seeing you read it.

3. Do not be afraid of marking it or of making marginal notes. Mark texts that contain promises, exhortations, warnings to sinners and to Christians, gospel invitations to the unconverted, and so on.

4. Set apart at least fifteen minutes a day or more for study and meditation. This will have great results and will never be regretted.

5. Prepare your heart to know the law of the Lord, and to do it. *For Ezra had set his heart to study the law of* *the LORD and to practice it, and to teach His statutes and ordinances in Israel* (Ezra 7:10).

6. Always ask God to open the eyes of your understanding that you may see the truth, and expect that He will answer your prayer.

7. Cast every burden of doubt upon the Lord. *Cast your burden upon the LORD and He will sustain you; He will never allow the righteous to be shaken* (Psalm 55:22). Do not be afraid to look for a reason for the hope that is in you. *But sanctify Christ as Lord in your hearts, always being ready to make a defense to everyone who asks you to give an account for the hope that is in you, yet with gentleness and reverence* (1 Peter 3:15).

8. Believe in the Bible as God's revelation to you, and act accordingly. Do not reject any portion because it contains the supernatural or because you cannot understand it. Reverence all Scripture. Remember how highly God views it.

> *The law of the LORD is perfect, restoring the soul; The testimony of the LORD is sure, making wise the simple. The precepts of the LORD are right, rejoicing the heart; The commandment of the LORD is pure, enlightening the eyes. The fear of the LORD is clean, enduring forever; The judgments of the LORD are true; they are righteous altogether. They are more desirable than gold,*

yes, than much fine gold; Sweeter also than
honey and the drippings of the honeycomb.
(Psalm 19:7-10)

9. Learn at least one verse of Scripture each day. Verses committed to memory will be wonderfully useful in your daily life and walk. *Your word I have treasured in my heart, that I may not sin against You* (Psalm 119:11). Some Christians can quote sports statistics or the songs of the world better than they can quote the Bible.

10. If you are a preacher or a Sunday school teacher, try at any cost to master your Bible. You ought to know it better than anyone in your congregation or class.

11. Strive to be exact in quoting Scripture.

12. Adopt some systematic plan of Bible study: either topical or by subjects, like "The Blood," "Prayer," "Hope," or by books of the Bible, or by some other plan outlined in the preceding pages.

13. Study to know for what and to whom each book of the Bible was written. Combine the Old Testament with the New. Study Hebrews and Leviticus together, the Acts of the Apostles and the Epistles, the prophets and the historical books of the Old Testament.

14. Study how to use the Bible so as to walk with God in closer communion. Also, study so as to gain a working knowledge of Scripture for leading others to Christ. An old minister used to say that the cries of neglected texts were always sounding in his ears, asking why he did not show how important they were.

15. Do not be satisfied with simply reading a chapter daily. *Study* the meaning of at least one verse.

> *For whatever was written in earlier times was written for our instruction, so that through perseverance and the encouragement of the Scriptures we might have hope.*
> (Romans 15:4)

About Dwight L. Moody

A Brief Description of the Life of the Author

Dwight Lyman Moody was born on February 5, 1837, in Northfield, Massachusetts. His father died when Dwight was only four years old, leaving his mother with nine children to care for. When Dwight was seventeen years old, he left for Boston to work as a salesman. A year later, he was led to Jesus Christ by Edward Kimball, Moody's Sunday school teacher. Moody soon left for Chicago and began teaching a Sunday school class of his own. By the time he was twenty-three, he had become a successful shoe salesman, earing $5,000 in only eight months, which was a lot of money for the middle of the nineteenth century. Having decided to follow Jesus, though, he left his career to engage in Christian work for only $300 a year.

D. L. Moody was not an ordained minister, but was an effective evangelist. He was once told by Henry

Varley, a British evangelist, "Moody, the world has yet to see what God will do with a man fully consecrated to Him."

Moody later said, "By God's help, I aim to be that man."

It is estimated that during his lifetime, without the help of television or radio, Moody traveled more than one million miles, preached to more than one million people, and personally dealt with over seven hundred and fifty thousand individuals.

D. L. Moody died on December 22, 1899.

Moody once said, "Some day you will read in the papers that D. L. Moody, of East Northfield, is dead. Don't you believe a word of it! At that moment I shall be more alive than I am now. I shall have gone up higher, that is all – out of this old clay tenement into a house that is immortal; a body that death cannot touch, that sin cannot taint, a body fashioned like unto His glorious body. I was born of the flesh in 1837. I was born of the Spirit in 1856. That which is born of the flesh may die. That which is born of the Spirit will live forever."

Similar Updated Classics by

THE
OVERCOMING
LIFE

But be ye doers
of the word, and
not hearers only,
deceiving your
own selves.
— James 1:22

DWIGHT L. MOODY

UPDATED EDITION

Are you an overcomer? Or, are you plagued by little sins that easily beset you? Even worse, are you failing in your Christian walk, but refuse to admit and address it? No Christian can afford to dismiss the call to be an overcomer. The earthly cost is minor; the eternal reward is beyond measure.

Dwight L. Moody is a master at unearthing what ails us. He uses stories and humor to bring to light the essential principles of successful Christian living. Each aspect of overcoming is looked at from a practical and understandable angle. The solution Moody presents for our problems is not religion, rules, or other outward corrections. Instead, he takes us to the heart of the matter and prescribes biblical, God-given remedies for every Christian's life. Get ready to embrace genuine victory for today, and joy for eternity.

Available where books are sold.

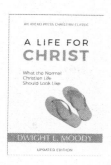

A LIFE FOR CHRIST

What the Normal
Christian Life
Should Look Like

DWIGHT L. MOODY

UPDATED EDITION

In the church today, we have everything buttoned up perfectly. The music is flawless, the sermon well-prepared and smoothly delivered, and the grounds meticulously kept. People come on time and go home on time. But a fundamental element is missing. The business of church has undermined the individual's need to truly live for Christ, so much so, that only a limited few are seeing their life impact the world.

Dwight L. Moody takes us deep into Scripture and paints a clear picture of what ought to be an individual's life for Christ. The call for each Christian is to become an active member in the body of Christ. The motive is love for the Lord and our neighbor. The result will be the salvation of men, women, and children everywhere.

Available where books are sold.

Often disguised as something that would help him, evil accompanies Christian on his journey to the Celestial City. As you walk with him, you'll begin to identify today's many religious pitfalls. These are presented by men such as Pliable, who turns back at the Slough of Despond; and Ignorance, who believes he's a true follower of Christ when he's really only trusting in himself. Each character represented in this allegory is intentionally and profoundly accurate in its depiction of what we see all around us, and unfortunately, what we too often see in ourselves. But while Christian is injured and nearly killed, he eventually prevails to the end. So can you.

The best part of this book is the Bible verses added to the text. The original Pilgrim's Progress listed the Bible verse references, but the verses themselves are so impactful when tied to the scenes in this allegory, that they are now included within the text of this book. The text is tweaked just enough to make it readable today, for the young and the old. Youngsters in particular will be drawn to the original illustrations included in this wonderful classic.

Available where books are sold.

Is humility a Christlike attribute that should be pursued? And even if it should be, can genuine humility actually be attained? Often so practical in application that it is overlooked, the answer is found by studying the life and words of Christ (*whosoever will be chief among you, let him be your slave*). This little book is a loud call to all committed Christians to prove that meekness and lowliness of heart is the evidence by which those who follow the meek and lowly Lamb of God are to be known. Never mind that your initial efforts will be misunderstood, taken advantage of, or even resisted. Instead, learn from the One who *came not to be ministered unto, but to serve.* For a Christian to be alive, for the life of Christ to reign in and through us, we must be empty of ourselves, exchanging our life for His life, our pride for true, Christlike humility.

Available where books are sold.

Donated by Prison Alliance
Write us a letter & enroll in
our PA Bible Study today!
PO Box 97095 Raleigh NC 27624